GO
BE YOU
TO THE
FULLEST

Finding and fulfilling your purpose

AYILERU ALIKOR MORTON

WESTBOW
PRESS®
A DIVISION OF THOMAS NELSON
& ZONDERVAN

WestBow Press books may be ordered through booksellers or by contacting:

WestBow Press
A Division of Thomas Nelson & Zondervan
1663 Liberty Drive
Bloomington, IN 47403
www.westbowpress.com
1 (866) 928-1240

ISBN: 978-1-5127-9433-5 (sc)
ISBN: 978-1-5127-9434-2 (e)

Library of Congress Control Number: 2017910988

Print information available on the last page.

WestBow Press rev. date: 7/28/2017

CONTENTS

DEDICATION

This book is dedicated to my Savior and friend Jesus Christ, my Comforter and teacher the Holy Spirit and my Lord and creator, God the Father.

Thank You LORD for loving me, and making something 'bea-u-ti-ful' out of my life. To God be all the glory and praise forevermore. Amen!

ACKNOWLEDGEMENTS

I would like to thank my husband and children, for their love, patience and encouragement throughout this process. Richard III and Stephen, thanks for your love which inspires me. Thank you Richard for your sacrifice and for giving me that extra push which I needed at those crucial times.

I am also grateful to my parents - Johnson and Philippa Alikor. Thank you for teaching me the fear of God very early in my life, without which I would not be where I am today, and for your love patience and dedication.

Many thanks go to my mentors and friends who never stopped praying for me until this baby was birthed; I appreciate your consistent inquiries and prayers which gave me that extra nudge to keep moving.

I also want to thank Lisa Leach for her hard work in editing this book. Thank you for all your help, advice and encouragement, you are a godsend.

It is with much gratitude that I acknowledge Dr. Friday Bekee of Gospel Power Ministry. Thank you for being a true leader, mentor and father, and for your continuous love and support.

INTRODUCTION

Have you ever wondered who you are and why you are here? Have you sometimes felt like you were different?

I have. As a young Christian in ministry, I struggled with my sense of identity and purpose. I know there are a lot of books out there written on "purpose." My intention is not to repeat or compete with what's already out there. Instead, in this book I have shared my struggles, along with some truths the Lord has given to help me overcome those struggles.

When I struggled with my purpose, it resulted in rejection and low self-esteem. These two are closely related; often rejection damages our self-esteem and that in turn leads to more rejection.

But if you know your purpose—who you are and why you are here—then self-esteem is no longer an issue. You begin to discover your unique qualities and gifts, who you are called to be and what you are called to do, and you begin to accept and love yourself, because you are BEAUTIFUL.

I started work on this book with the idea of encouraging young women. At the time, I was given a new way to look at the word "beautiful." We've all had so much pressure on us to focus on external beauty. However, I now understand that beauty is not based on material things. Nor is it about changing who you are. It is all about you just being YOU to the fullest: Be-YOU-to-FULL!

A butterfly begins life as an egg. You would hardly hear anyone gasp with admiration when looking at the egg of a butterfly. You probably wouldn't hear them saying how beautiful the larva is, either. Some might also be grossed out by the pupa, wrapped up and hidden away while the caterpillar undergoes its transformation. But after that butterfly fully develops, "beautiful" comes to mind all the time. So it is with us.

We go through many stages, and some may be nicer than others. But ultimately, "beautiful" is about you being all you can be as the one God created you to be. It's not about trying to be someone else. **Only you can be you!**

In each chapter, I address basic issues that are common to all of us. **That is, we all have a purpose, we all have a past, an identity, and gifts. We all go through seasons of preparation, we're all affected by time, and there is a need for each of us. We are all designed to thrive when coming into God's will, and there are specific ways to discover, bring to birth and nurture our purpose in life.** I share Scripture passages on each topic as well as stories from my own experience to highlight what God has shown me over the years.

A note on Scripture references: While researching this book, I discovered so many verses in the Bible on the subject of purpose. If each one of them were to be included in this book, you would be as amazed as I was. And if I were to expound on each one of them, this book would be too enormous to handle, therefore I have applied just a few.

A note on word meanings: Words communicate differently to different people. Many words are similar in nature and might be used interchangeably to convey the same message. In this book, when I talk about purpose or calling, some of the other words I use are: **Gifts, Talents, Goals, Vision, Dream, Cause, Mission, Journey, Destination, Destiny, Assignment, Calling, and Will.** The list goes on. They may not all mean the same thing, but they all play a part in describing your unique make-up.

My hope is that this book will help those who struggle with low self-esteem and rejection. I believe that if you are willing to embrace the process of discovering who you are and why you are here, you'll not only find out your purpose and specific calling in life, but you will also discover how to accept and love yourself ...because you are BEAUTIFUL.

So with this book I encourage you to *"Go, beautiful! – Go 'be you to 'full'!"* and find fulfillment in YOUR JOURNEY.

Ayileru Morton

CHAPTER 1

Your Purpose

Who has saved us, and called us with a holy calling, not according to our works, but according to His own purpose and grace which was given to us in Christ Jesus before time began. (2 Timothy 1:9)

Who am I? Why am I here? What am I to accomplish?
Everyone has a unique role in this world.
And everyone needs to know they have value and worth.
Do you know how valuable you are? Without this knowledge, we lose hope! We go about life with no zeal— nothing to look forward to, no reason to fight.
"Hope deferred makes the heart sick." (Proverbs 13:12)
We all need hope in our lives. We need a reason to get up in the morning...
My dad suffered a stroke few years ago. It left him with some paralysis on his left side. As difficult as it was, we were thankful because his right hand (his dominant hand) was not affected.
He loved to write, and even though he did not do a lot of writing after that, just knowing that he still *could* still gave him hope.

1

He spent months in rehabilitation. Those were very tough months for him, both physically and mentally.

He had to hold onto his reason to live.

You see, he had an elder sister who had taken care of him as a child, and he expressed a strong desire to always be there for her. He was determined that he would care for her and support her for as long as she lived. If nothing else, this determination alone kept him fighting.

Finally he came home to continue his recovery, was able to see his sister again, and fulfill his promise.

He had a reason to fight and that gave him hope. He had a purpose and a reason to get up in the morning, and it gave him strength and power to keep going.

...But indeed for this purpose I have raised you up, that I may show My power in you, and that My name may be declared in all the earth. (Exodus 9:16)

People with near-death experiences share that one of their main fears is leaving this life with incomplete assignments... unfinished business...

What is your assignment in this life?

Here's a general assignment:

God created us in His own image—and He told us to *have dominion and to be fruitful. (Genesis 1:26-30; 9:1-7).*

In addition to that general assignment, Christians have a more specific assignment: to *make disciples*—(the "Great Commission," Matthew 28:16-20). From this we can see that being fruitful involves our spiritual life as well. Fruitfulness is very important to the Lord, and He expressed this all through His word. We see it when He commands His people to pass on testimonies to future generations, and we also see it in many parables Jesus shared, such as the parable of the fig tree.

In addition to those general assignments, each one of us has a *personal* assignment—something that is unique to our lives. Our personal assignment still includes making disciples and being fruitful, but each of us may go about it in different ways.

Your assignment is yours alone; no one else can be you. No one else has your particular purpose and destiny.

The word "destiny" used to evoke feelings of fear in me, maybe because it made me feel I had no control over the course and outcome of my life. I now feel more at ease with that word when I look at it with the idea that I have a *"destination."* A destination is a place to which we are going, an end goal.

We each have a destination, a goal, a purpose.

You can view it this way: You can be headed to a specific place, but let's say you need to make certain stops before getting there. Or maybe you take certain turns along the way in order to get there. The fulfillment of one part of your purpose could lead to another, just like steps on a path or stairway help us get to a destination.

There was a time when David was a Shepherd boy, keeping his father's sheep and he was good at that. Then the time came when he became the King's armor bearer, then a soldier and warrior and finally, King of Israel. As he fulfilled his purpose on one level, he was set up for another, till he got to his main purpose as king.

Jesus began as a Carpenter, then a Rabbi-teacher and preacher of the Gospel, working miracles. Finally as the Savior he gave his life on the cross, resurrected on the third day. And now He is seated at the right hand of His Father.

You might be called to be a pastor, but maybe you need to go through other steps in your life; you might be a choir member, then a youth pastor...and finally a senior pastor.

Or let's say you are a church custodian at this time in your life; that does not mean that your dream of being a pastor will never manifest. If you are a cashier at a fast food restaurant right now, that doesn't mean you will never be a manager or own your own franchise.

Never despise small beginnings!

Hold onto that dream and purpose, just as Joseph did, and run till you get to the end, just like Paul did.

So we each have a destination. And we each have free will to choose how we get there.

Life might not be a straight line, but meanwhile....

"...we know that all things work together for good to those who love God, to those who are called according to His purpose." (Romans 8:28)

According to this verse, it is not *our* calling or our purpose; it is *His* calling and *His* purpose.

Furthermore God *"has saved us and called us with a holy calling, not according to our works, but according to* **His own purpose** *and grace which was given to us in Christ Jesus before time began..." (2 Timothy 1:9)*

What is purpose?

Dictionary.com gives one definition of purpose as *"the reason for which something exists, or is done, made, used..."*

If something has no purpose, it has no reason to exist and it needs to be tossed. (God forbid that from happening to our lives!)

The Bible says if salt loses its flavor (its usefulness or purpose), then it is good for nothing and needs to be thrown out. *(Matthew 5:13)* Jesus was referring to believers being the "salt of the earth"—may we keep our flavor and not become good for nothing!

You cannot live a fulfilled life without purpose or a vision. Eventually it will be a life of emptiness and misery. The Bible says, *"Without a vision the people perish." (Proverbs 29:18)* Having a vision helps you see your worth and value. It helps you know you are needed and knowing this keeps you focused on your purpose for life.

A while back, I came across a TV show in which people had to get help to have their houses cleaned out because they were in danger of being shut down by the health department. As I watched this program, I wondered why these individuals never threw anything out; they chose to hold onto everything, even when it got so bad that their homes became uninhabitable!

Then it occurred to me: They actually believed they *needed* those things. To them all their things were valuable for various reasons. No progress was made with their cleaning because they saw potential purpose in *all* of their possessions. They saw those things as being useful, if not presently, then sometime in the future...so they couldn't throw them out.

What to do? They had to adjust their vision. Up to that time they hadn't been able to decide what they truly needed and what they could do without.

In the same way, you have to find out what your purpose is in your life so that first, you can discern what is truly useful for that purpose, (not to mention view *yourself* as useful!) And second, so you won't have to hold onto *everything* and get all cluttered up like those people with the overwhelming mess in their houses.

That is, you cannot do *everything* in life or your days would be chaotic and unmanageable; you have to make some choices and let go of a few things. And your choices will need to be based on the vision for your life. If you know what you are called to be and do, then when it comes time to make choices, you won't throw yourself out in the process.

Will you know what to keep and what to throw out? You will, once you know your purpose.

So how do you find out your purpose?

It calls to you from within. Look within and you'll find that calling which God has placed inside of you. One reason many people go around searching for fulfillment is that they do not realize they will find it within. They think they can find it in outside themselves, often in material things like money, fame or relationships. God created you with your purpose embedded in you; that's why you feel a void on the inside when you haven't yet discovered it.

And by the way, you cannot wholly fulfill your purpose without God's help. After all, He is the one who put it inside of you. So look within, and look to Him. Let God help you find fulfilment and fullness.

And read this book!

You might find a treasure map with a few clues in here to help you discover your life's special assignment.

CHAPTER 2

Your Past

"Brethren, I do not count myself to have apprehended; but one thing I do, forgetting those things which are behind and reaching forward to those things which are ahead, I press toward the goal for the prize of the upward call of God in Christ Jesus." (Philippians 3:13 & 14)

Everyone has a past. And everyone's past is made up of positive and negative experiences.

Have you ever done something you're not proud of?

I believe we all have, at some point in our lives. Sometimes too, unexpected events throw us off course or cause us to stumble. The Bible says, *"A righteous man may fall seven times and rise again..."* (Proverbs 24:16)

There is victory in getting back up after you fall; furthermore in so doing you send a message to the enemy, letting him know that he is not your judge. God alone is Judge. He's also the Author and Finisher of your faith, the One enabling you to finish the race.

Some people are ashamed of their past and want nothing to do with it. However they fail to realize that their past has played a role in molding their lives, in forming who they are and who they are going to be. If they resist the past, they might also miss the stepping-stone it could be to their future.

Have you ever been encouraged by someone else's past struggles?

Often people have said to me, "I would rather hear from someone who has gone through what I am going through."

Why is that? The ones who are going through trials sense genuineness in those who have walked in their shoes. If they've lived through similar situations, they will likely be more understanding and less judgmental. They can relate more easily and have better insight into other's problems or situations. "Been there, done that," as you've heard people say.

Overcomers had to overcome something.

These people are often willing and able to share the steps they took to overcome.

This is not to say that those who have not walked in their shoes do not have the ability to help or advise others; they too can be wise and empathetic. But it is to say that nothing is wasted—especially your struggles.

If you have struggles, you may be very helpful to others one day.

On the other hand, I've also heard people say they would much rather listen to someone who did *not* have one of those big testimonies such as how they got delivered from drug and alcohol addiction. At first that struck me as surprising! But then I understood: Sometimes those "big" testimonies are so dramatic that it's easy to think that getting into trouble is the only way to end up with something to share.

Many times young kids (usually in their teens) have left the faith intentionally so as to acquire a big testimony. They've felt as though they have been "good" all their lives and therefore they have nothing to testify. They are convinced that their lives are void of these great deliverances – and therefore not interesting enough. Imagine that!

It's more common than you might think; we make the mistake of thinking everyone would rather hear about God delivering us from drug addiction, alcohol, promiscuity, or some other dramatically sinful behavior.

Often the ones who fall into this trap are children of pastors, ministers of the gospel, religious leaders or parents who are dedicated to ministry. In spite of all their striving to keep their children protected and shielded from the perils of the world, somehow their kids picked up a lopsided view of sin and salvation.

Do you think your life is uninteresting?

I've been there, done that. (Or *not* done that, as the case may be!)

There was a time I did not feel I had an "interesting testimony," having been sheltered all my life. Often I was tempted to yield to the peer pressure of doing drugs, just so I could acquire that kind of testimony.

My parents were very strict and religious. As a result, we were shielded from the world and a lot of negative habits. There were plenty of things that our peers were into; we were forbidden to do those things. So for the most part, my siblings and I did not get into any major trouble. We were viewed as being "good kids" (although far from it), and we were labeled as such because we did not get into drugs, drinking and so on.

However, staying away from those more obvious habits didn't make me good. In fact, if I thought I could be "good" on my own, I'd be in just as much danger of sinning by being smug and judgmental. I'm grateful that the Lord delivered me from this mindset!

Maybe you, too, have had these thoughts...

Do you feel that you are good because you have never

been addicted to drugs or committed an offence that landed you in jail?

Or do you feel that you do not have a testimony—that God has not delivered you from anything "big," so no one would be interested in listening to your testimony?

My prayer is that your eyes will be opened to the following truths:

First, there is only One Who is good, and that is God. So if we looked honestly into our lives, we would realize that we do fall short. There are things we've neglected to do, and there are things we have done that we may regret, things we may not be able to tell someone. There are things we struggle with and areas in which we need the Lord to help us.

Secondly, the fact that the Lord did not allow you get into drugs, armed robbery, promiscuity or some other major trouble is a testimony in itself. The Lord covered you and delivered you from evil. *"Lead me not into temptation but deliver me from evil..."* (from the Lord's Prayer, Matthew 6:13).

Deliverance is not just about getting out of trouble you've gotten into. It is also about being led away from temptation or evil in the first place.

It is time for us to view these as the great deliverances they are, and not feel that we have to make poor choices or get ourselves into dangerous situations or lifestyles with the thought that we would acquire a great testimony.

Look into your life and notice the stories of the Lord's deliverances. They do not have to sound like someone else's. Your testimony is just as important as someone else's and can help somebody. It's your past, it's your testimony, and it's your story.

Whether you feel like you've been "bad" OR think your past isn't exciting enough, either way the plan of the enemy is to attach negative memories from our past in order to drive you as far away as possible from your calling.

He'll have you focus on your failures, hurts and rejections—even on your lack of dramatic testimony—to keep you from envisioning God's future for you. Whenever he succeeds in doing this, know that God is already right there to help you forgive yourself. He is there to release you from the burden of the past and move you into His call for your life.

And the vessel that he made of clay was marred in the hand of the potter; so he made it again into another vessel, as it seemed good to the potter to make. (Jeremiah 18:4)

Do not put yourself in the path of danger just to have a testimony. You already have one!

For those who *have* been through excruciating circumstances, you might question why God allowed it. No one knows why, but God is able to use it to help someone along the way. Do you remember how Jesus told Peter to strengthen his brethren after he had repented?

You have a testimony too! Use it to strengthen someone!

For in that He Himself has suffered, being tempted, He is able to aid those who are tempted. (Hebrews 2:18)

God is the Potter and we are the clay; we cannot try to figure out the whys or hows, but we *can* choose to trust Him to reshape us as need be into vessels He can use.

MOSES

Moses had a past in Egypt. He'd murdered a man—an Egyptian who he witnessed beating a Hebrew. Moses had tried to answer his call in the best way he knew how. He'd been called to be a leader to help the Israelites get out of bondage, but had acted prematurely. That is, he'd attempted to "do God's will" on his own, without discerning God's leading in the matter.

After that first murder, on the second day he found two Hebrew men fighting. When he tried to intervene that time, one of the men said to him, *"Who made you a prince and a judge over us?"* (Exodus 2:14)

Moses fled because he was afraid; Pharaoh intended to kill him. At that point he had a past, not one that made him proud.

First murder, then betrayal and rejection...

Fast-forward forty years: Moses has an encounter with God, and God sends him back to confront his past so as to fulfill his call—the call he knew was on his life as a young child but had tried to fulfill in his own way. The call that had everything to do with the words that were used to mock him by his fellow Hebrew.

Needless to say, Moses was reluctant to be a leader after the results of that first attempt, but God didn't back down.

Moses was not the only one who tried to run away from his past. There was another man who tried to fulfill his call in his own way but ended up messing things up. His name was Jacob.

JACOB

Let's take a look at Jacob's past: When Esau and Jacob were still in the womb, their mother, Rebekah, received a prophecy: *"Two nations are in your womb, Two peoples shall be separated from your body; One people shall be stronger than the other, And the older shall serve the younger."* (Genesis 25:23)

However just like Moses, Jacob also acted prematurely and schemed a way to do things without waiting on God.

First he bought Esau's birthright, and later with the help of his mother, he stole Esau's blessing. He had to leave home because he feared for his life. But again we see God's intervention; after so many years, God tells Jacob to go back home.

Jacob had run away from his calling because a negative experience had been attached to it. It was not easy for him to go back home to face his older brother, but God intervened and helped him turn around. **Our past—even the negative stuff—plays a part in shaping our future.** So we do not need to run from or deny our past.

In addition to those people who run (or try to run) from their past, there are also those who dwell *too much* on their past. Lot's wife was one who wanted to stay in her past, and as a result she lost the opportunity to move into where God wanted to take her.

LOT'S WIFE

Abraham's nephew Lot dwelt in Sodom. When the outcry against Sodom and its rampant sin had grown great before His face, God sent angels to destroy the city. The angels warned Lot, his wife and kids and led them away from the city. The family was instructed not to look behind nor stay anywhere in the plain.

But Lot's wife looked back. And when she did, she turned into a pillar of salt. Her inability to focus on God's plan—His good future full of peace and hope for her and her family—led to a disastrous end for her. She turned into a pillar of salt. Not exactly useful! If we focus on what's behind us and not on God's future for us, we get stuck, ineffective and unfruitful! We lose our flavor! We are the salt of the earth and cannot afford to lose our flavor. Jesus clearly states that when salt loses its flavor it is then good for nothing.

It is crucial that you not to allow your past to hold you back. At times you may be directed by God to address certain issues from the past, such as when He is healing and redeeming those times in your life. But do not brood on it indefinitely; do not focus backward or dwell on past mistakes, bondages, or regrets.

If you keep looking behind, you become so focused on the past that you cannot see what's ahead of you. You lose vision and momentum. You become stuck, paralyzed like Lot's wife, unable to move forward.

As mentioned earlier, once you feel useless or purposeless, you lose the drive to keep on living. Do not allow past failures or mistakes to occupy the room that belongs to your goals and visions.

Some people think it is okay to dwell on past good exploits, but no matter how good or bad your past has been, dwelling on it makes you lose focus on the future.

The best way to deal with your past—good or bad—is to not run from it, not dwell on it, but *learn* from it.

Yes, it contributes a great deal in shaping you, but it's not where you'll want to stay.

When God uses you to do exploits, rejoice in Him, testify of Him but do not dwell there. Remember how He helped you overcome, but also move on to new goals and new exploits God has in store for you. Do not be complacent or comfortable with where you are. Go higher in God, do not stay anywhere in the plain.

Do not remember the former things, nor consider the things of old. Behold, I will do a new thing, Now it shall spring forth; Shall you not know it? I will even make a road in the wilderness and rivers in the desert. (Isaiah 43:18 & 19)

The Bible tells us of a man who neither ran away from his past nor dwelt on it; instead he embraced it, learned from it and moved into higher victories in God. This young man was faced with a situation where he could have denied his past or hidden it, because it did not measure up to those around him. However he chose not to.

He was mocked by his older siblings, the king doubted him and his adversary laughed at him; yet all these did not deter him. He still chose to use what he had learned from his past to defeat his giant. Who was this man?

DAVID

If you guessed David, you are right on. As I mentioned in the previous chapter, David chose to go to battle in his shepherd's clothing and with his proven—though unconventional— equipment rather than in the King's armor.

Let's put this into perspective: The typical warrior of his day had a brass helmet, a shield the size of a door, a coat of mail, a sword, javelins and spears—but David had his staff, a shepherd's bag (scrip), stones and a sling.

Saul's army consisted of experienced soldiers, but David was an experienced shepherd.

In other words, your gifts might not *look* superior compared to others around you, but that does not make them less effective or less valuable. Notice that David did not try to change into an experienced soldier; he chose to be an experienced shepherd.

Do not try to be someone else; aim to be a better you.

David had not tested the soldiers' equipment, but he sure had tested his own equipment. And he had a testimony as a shepherd: *"The LORD, who delivered me from the paw of the lion and from the paw of the bear, He will deliver me from the hand of this Philistine."* (I Samuel 17:37)

Furthermore, David knew that what mattered most was not his background or his outfit, but the fact that God was with him. God had already delivered David in previous situations and used the skills, gifts and temperament He had given him; David knew God would deliver him again using those same gifts—sharpened and shaped through his past experiences.

Do not run away from your past or your identity. Like David, pick up the smooth stones from the dirt, put them in your bag and use them to fight your Goliath.

Pick out the lessons you have learned from your past— good or bad—and use them to win bigger battles in the future.

If you are having doubts about a current situation you are facing, do not focus on how you failed in the past. Do not focus on your equipment either. Focus on the fact that God is with you and that He who brought you to it will surely bring you through it.

THE WOMAN AT THE WELL

We cannot forget the story of the woman whose past the Lord used to reach a whole city. Jesus met her at the well where she was drawing water at high noon. While talking with her, He asked her to go get her husband--to which she replied that she had none.

He acknowledged her honesty, because she had five husbands in the past and presently was with one who was not her husband. The Samaritan woman, after she perceived that Jesus was a prophet, went into the city and testified all about Him: *"Come, see a Man who told me all things that I ever did! Could this be the Christ?" (John 4:29)*

The Samaritan woman might have felt like hiding at first; the very reason she was at the well at noon was because it was when no one else would be there. However as Jesus ministered to her, she ended up not hiding her past but using it as a testimony to minister to a city.

Let the Lord use your past!

Originally I come from Nigeria. When we prepare one of our main rice dishes, we would go through the rice before cooking to separate the rice from stones. We refer to this process as "picking rice."

One day as I looked back over my life, complaining (I must confess) over pains and bad experiences I had gone through, the Lord began to minister to me. He reminded me that just as we had to separate rice from stones, I needed to pick out the good, learn from it and throw out the bad.

I took His advice. When I did just that, joy flooded my spirit; instead of being bitter, I was thankful. Whenever you remember your past, pick up the good--the lessons and the blessings--and throw out the stones. You might be surprised to find out how many great people have "bad" things in their lives. Just possibly, they became great by separating the rice from the stones.

GREATNESS IS IN YOU

Do you have a desire to be great? This is wonderful because there is greatness in all of us, but most people misunderstand what 'greatness' truly means. What is the true meaning of greatness? How do you discover the greatness within you?

Greatness does not depend on your past—which family you were born into, what mistakes you made, or your physical appearance, how handsome or beautiful you are.

Some think they'll never be great because of their past mistakes or because their parents are not rich or famous enough. But look at David; he was from a humble unknown home, he was the youngest and least expected in his family (I Samuel 16:11), but he became a great king.

I could give you lots of examples from the Bible, along with real life examples of people who became great regardless of their past. Greatness is not just standing before a million people to preach, singing in front of a sold-out crowd, becoming the President of a country, or becoming the richest man in the world.

Greatest is maximizing your potential. It is allowing God to use you in service to *your* full potential.

The Bible says, *"... whoever desires to become great among you shall be your servant." (Mark 10:43)* Greatness has a lot to do with service. If you want to be great, then you have to be ready to serve, to your full potential. What is your full potential?

Your full potential is on the inside. It could be different from someone else's, but that does not make it inferior or less important. Some people feel they have to be like someone else to be considered great; in their minds, if they preach, sing, draw, dance or write like a particular person with a big

18

name, then they would be convinced that they are great or being used mightily by God.

This belief is a misconception.

When you were created, God placed your calling or purpose within you. There is no one else like you!

Because of this blueprint that God places in each of us, even at a very young age children have a vision of what they want to do. They might not be able to articulate it or communicate exactly what they see themselves doing or becoming, but on some level they know.

They may try to relate it to something familiar—something they have experienced in their environment—but if that is lacking, sometimes confusion sets in. You might hear them say the words, "I don't know"— not because they do not know what they want to become, but because they cannot relate it to anything they've seen yet.

At other times the fear of failure could set in, the fear that they might not be able to accomplish their vision or purpose. We talked about Moses earlier; I believe that as a young child growing up, although he was brought up by the Egyptians, down deep he knew why he was born. He'd been taught early by his Hebrew mother, and he knew why he was created on this earth. That is why he reacted in the way he did, although prematurely at first.

Greatness is not measured by what you have, but how you use what you have.

As Christians we need to discover and nurture the gifts and callings God has placed in us because they have been placed in us according to the grace given to us.

* *For I say, through the grace given to me, to everyone who is among you, not to think of himself more highly than he ought to think, but to think soberly, as God has dealt to **each one a measure of faith**.*

19

Having then gifts differing according to the grace that is given to us, let us use them: if prophecy, let us prophesy in proportion to our faith. (Romans 12:3-8)

- *There are diversities of gifts, but the same Spirit. There are differences of ministries, but the same Lord. And there are diversities of activities, but it is the same God who works all in all. But the manifestation of the Spirit **is given to each one for the profit of all**: for to one is given the word of wisdom through the Spirit, to another the word of knowledge through the same Spirit, to another faith by the same Spirit, to another gifts of healings by the same Spirit, to another the working of miracles, to another prophecy, to another discerning of spirits, to another different kinds of tongues, to another the interpretation of tongues. But one and the same Spirit works all these things, distributing to each one individually as He wills. (I Corinthians 12:4-11)*

We have been given different gifts, and within those gifts there are different graces. For example, there are people with the gift of prophecy, however amongst them there are different measures or levels of faith. God might have given you the grace to prophesy to thousands, and give to someone else the grace to prophesy to hundreds. You are to use your gifts according to the grace given to you.

Greatness is not about the numbers of people who come to hear you prophesy. Greatness is ministering or serving, using what you have to the full.

And have you noticed? **All the great people we admire have a past—and none of them stayed there, but moved forward to pursue their future.**

CHAPTER 3

Your Identity

For I delight in the law of God according to the inward man. But I see another law in my members, warring against the law of my mind, and bringing me into captivity to the law of sin which is in my members. O wretched man that I am! Who will deliver me from this body of death? I thank God—through Jesus Christ our Lord! ... Romans 7:22-25

"For You formed my inward parts; You covered me in my mother's womb.... Your eyes saw my substance, being yet unformed. And in Your book they all were written, the days fashioned for me, when as yet there were none of them." (Psalm 139:13, 16)

"Before I formed you in the womb, I knew you." (Jeremiah 1:5)

Pilate therefore said to Him, "Are You a king then?" Jesus answered, "You say rightly that I am a king. For this cause I was born, and for this cause I have come into the world, that I should bear witness to the truth. Everyone who is of the truth hears My voice." (John 18:37) ...Jesus knew who He was and why He came.

Everyone has a unique identity.

For many years I searched for a friend who would love me for *who I was.*

There were times I thought to myself, "There has to be someone out there who could be a friend to me, who could love me for who I am."

I had been through so many heartbreaks and so much hurt; I longed to be understood and loved. I heard many people talk about close friends, best friends, friends who were like siblings to them. I felt I didn't have that.

I tried to find a true friend who would love the real me. I was so focused on finding a true friend that I lost focus on finding the real me. Preoccupied with looking for that friend who would love me for who I was, still I had no idea who I was!

In the previous chapter, I mentioned the group of people who could not find fulfillment because they had no idea who they were. This is more common than we might think; there are huge numbers of people who have yet to discover their identity. They haven't yet become fully acquainted with themselves—their likes, their dislikes, their gifts and so on.

That was me.

While many struggle, as I did, with not knowing who they are, others struggle with knowing but not liking. In other words, they fight with their identity and wish they could be someone other than themselves. Sometimes people may experience a mixture of both.

Once I met a young lady who expressed great interest in becoming a veterinarian. A couple of years later I ran into her again, and to my surprise she expressed uncertainty about her career choice. After I inquired some more, she admitted that her previous choice had come from her parents. Even though she loved animals, she had no desire to be a veterinarian. At this point she felt lost.

My advice to her? Stick to what you love doing—your

interests, your heart's desire. It does not matter if it is different from everyone else's, or if it does not fit into a particular mold according to someone else's expectations.

Whatever your dream or desire is, it is significant.

What causes these identity struggles? I've observed that like the young lady above, many people have had lots of influences on their upbringing; they've been told what to do, what to like, what to dislike.

There is nothing wrong with guiding children; we are supposed to train our children when they are young. However as they grow up and show maturity, they should be given some responsibility in their decision-making process as well as opportunities to own their actions. That way they will get a clearer sense of who they are without automatically conforming to someone else's standard. They'll have a chance to discover who they are while still young.

If you don't know yourself well yet, it's not too late.

Ask yourself, "Who am I?"

To be acquainted with your individuality and unique characteristics is not selfish but essential for fulfilling your role in the world.

If you still think that focus on your identity isn't as important as other things, take a look at some of the questions God asks people in the Bible:

"What is your name?"

"What do you have in your hands?"

"Whose son are you?"

Or you may consider the questions these people ask when they are receiving a visit from Heaven and charged with a life-altering role to play:

"But who am I...?"

"How can I, since I am only...?"

These questions of identity are central to major turning points in the lives of biblical characters.

As you ponder these questions, you might want to take another look at Jacob and his encounter with the Angel of the Lord, Moses at the site of the burning bush, and David standing before Saul after slaying Goliath.

Also consider Gideon speaking with the angel of the Lord, or Mary during her visitation with the angel Gabriel. I've touched on their stories in this chapter, but I encourage you to read them first hand and see what you think.

In all these stories, I believe you'll find that identity is key to each one's destiny.

Now ask yourself: Is it possible to know where you are going without knowing where you are? In large shopping malls or museums they have maps with a red dot or arrow that says, "You are HERE."

That's because you can't navigate where you're going without knowing where you are.

In the same vein, **it's impossible to know your purpose without knowing your identity**. This is the reason God dealt first with the issue of identity in the lives of His children before He revealed His purpose for their lives. Not only that, but He went over it in greater detail for those who struggled with their identity.

MOSES

In chapter 2, we looked at Moses in the light of his past. During Moses' encounter at the site of the burning bush, however, the Lord had Moses' *future* in mind. It was there that God revealed his assignment: Moses had been chosen to deliver God's people from Pharaoh. But before Moses could embark on this mission, the Lord had to deal with the issue of Moses' identity.

When Moses asked the Lord, "Who am I, that I should

go to Pharaoh?" the Lord's answer was, "I will certainly be with you."

As you can see, the Lord was trying to convey to Moses that what mattered most was that He was with him.

Then Moses posed another question: "What do I say if they ask me what your name is?" At this point, while Moses knew that the Lord was going to be with him, he still needed to know who the Lord was.

The Lord said, "Tell them I AM sent you, the God of your fathers Abraham, Isaac, and Jacob."

"What if they do not believe *me*?" asked Moses. Notice, he did not ask, "What if they don't believe *You*?" Once again Moses was focused on who *he* was; he faced doubts over his identity, especially when it concerned the question of being accepted or believed by Pharaoh and his own people back in Egypt.

At that point the Lord asked him, *"What is that in your hand?"*

Moses had a shepherd's rod in his hand. It was plain as day. Did the Lord not know what was in the hand of Moses? Of course He knew.

But by asking this question, God reinforced Moses' identity: Although the rod (or staff) identified who Moses was at that point—a shepherd—God had plans to use him to fulfill his larger life purpose as a leader of Israel.

In his answer to God's question lay the revelation of who Moses was—a shepherd, yet on a different level than before; Moses' rod was a tool of his ministry and his purpose, both physically and spiritually.

Even with that revelation, he had a free choice to surrender. And Moses could not carry out the assignment that the Lord had for him without the knowledge and acceptance of his identity. Moses needed to know who he was in addition to knowing *whose* He was.

You cannot carry out your assignment (fulfill your purpose) on your own. You need the Lord and you need to know Him.

Even Paul, after he'd already encountered God and mentored many in the faith, prayed fervently *"...that I may know Him and the power of His resurrection, and the fellowship of His sufferings, being conformed to His death..."* (Philippians 3:10)

You need to know your true identity (as a Christian, your identity is in Christ). Without that knowledge, you run the risk of striving to be someone else, thinking that then and only *then* can God use you. Realize who you are and surrender who you are to the Lord; submit to Him and He will fulfill His purpose in you.

As Christians, our struggle with identity extends into our need to understand who God is. That is, the question of who we are is incomplete without knowing Whose we are:

- We are Children of God, a chosen generation, a royal priesthood. (I Peter 2:9)
- We are fearfully and wonderfully made. (Psalm 139:14)
- We are given dominion over every creature, given a charge to be fruitful and to multiply. (Gen 1:26-30)
- We are to be fruitful and multiply not only physically but spiritually as well. (Mark 16:15)

These are just a few of the things that show how thoroughly our identity is interwoven with God's.

JACOB

In Genesis 32:24, the Bible tells us that a Man wrestled with Jacob until the breaking of day. Now most Bible scholars say Jacob wrestled with the Lord. Whether it was the Lord or one of His angels, most of us can agree that the person was not human but a supernatural being.

Jacob wrestled with this Man, got his hip knocked out of joint in the process, but still wrestled until the Man pleaded with Jacob to let him go.

"I will not let you go unless you bless me," Jacob responded.

At that point the Man asked him, *"What is your name?"*

We are all aware that this Man, being supernatural, had to have known Jacob's name. So again, what was the purpose of the question?

The name Jacob means "Supplanter," meaning one who takes the place of another through schemes. So Jacob was a schemer!

All his life he was inclined to achieve things by schemes, not through dependence on God. Twice he supplanted his brother, and then he schemed a way to best his uncle. Finally when he came to the end of himself and realized that he could no longer continue scheming his way through, he surrendered to God. In facing the question of his name, he acknowledged who he was. ("You are HERE.")

And with that, he finally received his blessing: a *new* name—Israel—which means "who prevails with God." Jacob received a new identity in God.

There are others in the Bible who had identity questions. In 1 Samuel 9:21, we read about Saul who wondered why the prophet Samuel addressed him the way he did, considering that he was from the least tribe in Israel and his family was the least of all the families. Saul didn't yet have a sense of his own identity in the Lord.

In Judges 6: 15, during a conversation in which the Lord had hailed Gideon by saying, "Greetings, mighty warrior!" Gideon responded to the Lord, *"How can I save Israel? Indeed my clan is the weakest in Manasseh, and I am the least in my father's house."* Gideon, too, had no sense of who he was called to be or who God was promising to be for him.

In Luke 1:26, the angel Gabriel was sent by God to a young virgin. He greeted Mary and told her that she would be the mother of the Jesus, the Son of God. Like both Saul and Gideon, she had questions. She asked, *"How can this be, since I do not know a man?"* Gabriel explained how it would happen and assured her that *with God* nothing is impossible. Mary was yet to discover how favored she truly was.

None of these biblical characters saw themselves as God saw them. Each of them questioned their true identity in some way. But just as we witnessed with Moses, the Lord's answer to each of them was clear in its emphasis on *God's* identity, both with and for them. He replied to Gideon, "Surely I will be with you, and you shall defeat the Midianites as one man." And Gabriel's first greeting to Mary revealed the key to her identity in the Lord: "Rejoice, highly favored *one,* the Lord *is* with you."

Once again we see how God being *with* us and for us is key to the fulfillment of our purpose.

You were bought at a price; do not become slaves of men. Brethren, let each one remain with God in that state in which he was called. (1 Corinthians 7: 23 & 24)

PUT ON YOUR OWN GARMENTS

Speaking of true identities, the story of David stands out for me. I received some deeper revelation on his story while working on this book. As you may recall from the last chapter, David declined to fight in Saul's heavy armor, the reason being that he had not proved that equipment. David was simply conveying that it did not fit who he was; he had an identity already and was not going to deny it to embrace a new identity, one he had not proved.

In his past, he had encountered a lion and a bear (situations that threatened to devour him and his flock), but God brought him through with the weapons He had given him already (his gifts and experience). It took strength of character for David to do the more unconventional thing when facing Goliath, but because he had a clear sense of identity, that strength was readily available to him.

Some people might attempt to clothe you with their identity. It might even look impressive and necessary, the way Saul's armor did when it came to facing the giant. But as you commit to fulfilling your purpose or calling, be as bold as David. You can thank these people kindly, but let them know you cannot accept it because you have not proved it. It isn't yours.

Your identity is significant.

What's more, it's *yours*! Embrace it.

When David defeated Goliath, he had double assurance: He had his personal experience, and he also had the knowledge that the God of Abraham, Isaac and Jacob was with him. Together these two helped forge and strengthen his true identity.

Knowing who you are doesn't mean you won't be engaged in an ongoing journey in your life or have projects with challenges. There may be times of assessment and reassessment as you go through different chapters.

When you begin a journey or a project, you must take into account what you have and what you will need to ensure you have enough to accomplish your goal. For instance, if you want to build a house, first you will need to find out how much it will cost, then see if there's enough and what more you might require.

Just as you must start where you are, you must begin with what you have.

WHAT DO YOU HAVE NOW?

The story of Elisha and the widow teaches us this point. The widow had accumulated so much debt that the creditor was about to take her two sons as slaves.

Elijah said to her, *"Tell me, what do you have in your house?"* (2 Kings 4:2) This question is similar to the one God asked Moses. Take stock of what you have, and find out what you'll need to ensure you complete your goal.

What do you have in your life to fulfill your purpose? Who are you and what has God put in you?

You might view it as not being much, but it is significant.

It will make a difference if you first acknowledge it and then trust God to make up whatever you feel is lacking. Look what He did with just one boy's lunch—five loaves and two fishes—he fed over 5,000 people!

Jesus posed this question to his disciples: *"For which of you, intending to build a tower, does not sit down first and count the cost, whether he has enough to finish it?"* (Luke 14:28) In order to know if you have enough to build the tower, you must know what you have. Who are you? What do you have? Do not deny it; rather, use it to help build that tower.

As you consider all that makes up YOU—your background, your experiences, even your personality quirks—think about this: God has put you in your family for a reason; you were born to those parents for a reason; the experiences and struggles you went through were for a reason.

All these make up YOU, and you need all these components to complete your journey. You might even view all these different aspects of your life as tools in your toolbox, equipping you for your journey.

Our identity is a main target of enemy attack. This is because he knows we'll be unstoppable once we know who and Whose we are. As you may have noticed, many biblical accounts of encounters with the Lord begin with addressing the issue of identity.

God knew just how to handle each situation in which people struggled to embrace their identity and put their trust in Him.

He said to Gideon, "...*have I not sent you?*" (Judges 6:14)

And He said to Moses, *"Who has made man's mouth?"* (Exodus 4:11)

He turned their attention away from what they viewed as their weakness and directed them to focus on His strength.

When the enemy begins to attack, he figures if he can crush your identity, then he has gotten to you. He begins in the mind to try to destroy your self-worth. Notice that many people who hurt themselves or others are those who struggle with their self-worth. They have low self-esteem, do not yet like themselves or believe in themselves.

If you struggle in this way, do not be discouraged. Put your confidence in God and in whom He has made you to be. God knows all about you. Your true identity is in God. Is there anything too hard for Him?

If you do not believe in yourself anymore, focus on believing in God and who He is.

WHO GOD SAYS YOU ARE

As we end this chapter, take a journey with me to the beginning... The enemy tempted Eve by asking her a question. That question was intended to lure her into a conversation that would inject doubt about her identity into her mind.

It started off sounding innocent: *"Has God indeed said...?"* (Genesis 3:1) But then came a little twist: *"For God knows that in the day you eat of it your eyes will be opened and you will be like God...* (Genesis 3:5)

Notice how the focus shifted, and caused Eve to forget that she was *already* created "like God" –that is, made in God's image. (Genesis 1:26-28) Also, she was created to be Adam's helpmate, not his lord. (Genesis 2:20-23) On all counts, the serpent made her doubt who she was created to be.

He convinced her that she was not good enough; she had to be like someone else in order to excel and be content. The fruit was *"desirable to make one wise."* (v.6) Eve fell right into the trap. Made in God's image; she was *already* created to be wise! She did not embrace who God made her to be, therefore in that moment she doubted both Him *and* herself.

Are you in a position where you are doubting who God created you to be?

Guard your mind against those thoughts that would propel you into low self-esteem.

When the enemy begins to whisper doubts about your identity, remind him of the truth: You are "fearfully and wonderfully made" in God's image, and that makes you beautiful.

You do not need to be like someone else. If you feel you do not like yourself because of something you view as a weakness or failure, the first step is admitting that the problem exists, not denying it. Then surrender it to the One who created you and knows best how to help you overcome. Believe and be confident in God and who He made you to be. He loves you and He is able!

Fast forward into the New Testament: After the enemy had succeeded in getting the first Adam to fall, and he proceeded to use the same tactics on the second Adam—Jesus.

So he began in his usual serpentine way: *"If you are the son of God..."* (Luke 4:3)

Seriously—*If*?

He *was* the Son of God! (And still is!)

This temptation in the desert came *immediately after* Jesus' baptism in the Jordan where God had declared, *"This is my beloved son in whom I am well pleased."* (Matthew 17:5) Can't get any clearer than that!

Jesus knew who He was and He knew His purpose, so He did not fall for the enemy's attempts to cast doubt on His identity. Furthermore He didn't rely on His own resources either but went straight to God: For every temptation thrown at Him, Jesus reminded the enemy what the Word of God said.

For every weapon of doubt the enemy threw at Him, Jesus had a more powerful weapon – the Word of Truth—to counteract it.

Imagine if Eve or Adam had come back with God's Word when the enemy began his scheme to cause them to fall. *God's word* is a *God sword*; use it! When the enemy begins to flood your mind with doubts of who God has created you to be, remind him of the Word of God. That is your standard. Remind him of what God has said concerning you, and you will be strengthened in your God-given identity.

CHAPTER 4

Your Gifts

"Therefore I remind you to stir up the gift of God which is in you through the laying on of my hands. For God has not given us a spirit of fear, but of power and of love and of a sound mind." (2 Timothy 1:6-7)

There are diversities of gifts, but the same Spirit. There are differences of ministries, but the same Lord. And there are diversities of activities, but it is the same God who works all in all. But the manifestation of the Spirit is given to each one for the profit of all:

(1 Corinthians 12: 4-7)

Everyone has gifts.

When I realized that I was not gifted to sing, I packed my bags for a journey down the road of self-pity. On this journey, I complained to the Lord and asked Him why I was given no gifts. I told him how terrible it was that I could not sing, dance, preach or speak.

"It's not fair!" I whined. "Why is it that I have no gifts?"

I wish I could tell you that my complaining was short lived or that the journey was a brief one. I *can* tell you one thing though; it was on this journey that I discovered a powerful truth:

No one is brought into this world without gifts.

While some gifts are obvious or popular, other gifts have to be searched for a little deeper. However that does not make those gifts any less. If anything, they may be more precious. When we have to search harder for something, we often value it even more.

WHAT ARE GIFTS?

According to Merriam-Webster, a gift can be defined as *something given to another person; a special ability, a notable talent or capacity.*

The kind of gifts I am referring to in this chapter are talents as well as spiritual gifts. Both kinds of gifts play a vital part in your life purpose. My definition of "gift" is something you're good at through no strength or merit of your own.

When people are asked how they are able to sing or dance so well, their answer may be, "It is a gift." Meaning, they were born with it; they did not earn it or purchase it. I once heard a comedian define a gift as something you do the absolute best with the least amount of effort. That sums it up!

So if a gift is something you are given, then it's not something for which you'd take credit. You didn't earn it. And the minute it becomes earned it ceases to be a gift; it is then a payment or reward.

Acknowledging this fact puts things in perspective; it helps us have the right attitude when faced with either discouragement or a temptation to boast. Either way, all the glory goes to God.

Yes, we have the opportunity to develop the gift, but God first gave it to us to develop.

When I think of gifts, I think of giving God thanks first; **GIFT** = **G**od **I**s **F**irst **T**hanked! (Colossians 3:17)

The Bible says in 1 Corinthians 12:4 that there are diversities of gifts but the same Spirit, and different ministries but the same Lord. God has given all people various gifts to enable them fulfill their purpose in life. He has given us gifts to help us with our journey.

Not everyone is called to preach; neither is everyone called to sing. Not everyone is called to be a teacher; neither is everyone called to be a president. Not everyone is given the gift of prophecy or healings. We all have diverse gifts; the fact that someone may have more gifts than you does not make you less important.

There are instances in the Bible where we see individuals given great abilities at different levels, but they remained humble and did not elevate themselves above others.

Moses was one of those individuals; he was a great leader and yet the Bible refers to him as being *"more humble than all men who were on the face of the earth."* (Numbers 12:3)

Abigail is another example. She is described as woman of good understanding and beautiful appearance. Unfortunately she also had a rich husband who behaved very crudely. She could have acted like it was all his problem, but when she heard how her husband had treated David and his men, she went to David, humbled herself and asked for forgiveness. (I Samuel 25:2-35).

True humility is not about being less confident. It is about being confident in who you are and Whose you are.

If you want to be great in the kingdom of heaven, then *humility* is the key. (Matthew 8:4)

PITY PARTY VS. SWELLED HEAD

The Bible exhorts us not to think of ourselves more highly than we ought to, but to think soberly as God has dealt to each one a measure of faith. (Romans 12:3)

Furthermore, Jesus admonished the disciples when they disputed who would be the greatest; if anyone desired to be first, they had to be the last and the servant of all. (Mark 9:34-35)

In other words, the amount or size of your gift does not make you great, but rather how it is used in service to others. Your focus should never be on the gifts but on God who chooses to use you to reach out to others.

Thus says the LORD:
"Let not the wise man glory in his wisdom,
Let not the mighty man glory in his might,
Nor let the rich man glory in his riches;
But let him who glories glory in this,
That he understands and knows Me,
That I am the LORD, exercising loving kindness,
judgment, and righteousness in the earth.
For in these I delight," says the LORD.
(Jeremiah 9: 23-24)

Do you think God uses you in a small way only? Do you wish, like I did, that you could be used in some other, "bigger" way? Do you think of your gift as only a small thing?

The Scripture says, *"For who has despised the day of small things?" (Zechariah 4:10)*

Small things aren't bad in God's sight. If you trust God with little things, you will prepare yourself well to trust Him for larger things.

If you cannot believe God in small situations then it will be difficult, if not impossible to believe Him in bigger situations. In the same vein, if He cannot trust us with small assignments then how will he trust us with greater ones?

You see, God wants to help us believe in Him, so He entrusts us with small things first. That way we will be strengthened in faith and ready to be entrusted with bigger things. It takes faith to believe God and faith has to be developed. The way you develop faith is by using it, just as our muscles are developed by exercise.

The more you exercise your faith, the more it develops.

The same principle applies to talents; you develop your talents and gifts by using them in whatever situation you find yourself.

Notice I did not say, "using them only in those situations that are really important and high-profile."

No, I said, "...*whatever* situations you find yourself."

Those situations might seem small and unimportant to you, but they are important to God. When you look around the world, there are different ministries, large and small; larger ministries may have started small and later developed.

Furthermore a ministry's size does not determine its effectiveness – the fact that a ministry is large does not make it more important than a smaller ministry. A ministry or gift can be small and yet be significant and effective.

"For I say, through the grace given to me, to everyone who is among you, not to think of himself more highly than he ought to think, but to think soberly, as God has dealt to each one a measure of faith. For as we have many members in one body, but all the members do not have the same function, so we, being many, are one body in Christ, and individually members of one another. Having then gifts differing according to the grace that is given to us, let us use them: if prophecy, let us prophesy in proportion to our faith; or ministry, let us use it in our ministering; he who

teaches, in teaching; he who exhorts, in exhortation; he who gives, with liberality; he who leads, with diligence; he who shows mercy, with cheerfulness." (Romans 12:3-8)

THERE'S ENOUGH FOR EVERYBODY

God gave us the ability to move in ministry or gifts according to His grace. Although we are members of the same body, our gifts are different and are given to us in different proportions. Although some gifts are similar, no two gifts or callings are identical, just as no two individuals are identical. Even identical twins have something that differentiates them.

There have been presidents; there have been kings; there have been preachers... however no two presidents ever pursued the exact same cause. Similar causes, maybe. No two kings ever accomplished the exact same goals. Similar goals, maybe. No two preachers ever had the exact same vision. Similar visions or messages, maybe.

Have you ever considered what this world would be like if everyone were the same?

If everyone were a lawyer, if everyone were a doctor, or a president, or a farmer?

You do not have to think too hard before realizing it would be a disaster.

The Apostle Paul asks some great questions in Romans 12:17 to illustrate God's amazing variety: *"If the whole body was an eye, where would be the hearing?"* And in verse 29, *"Are all apostles? Are all prophets? Are all teachers?"* If everyone were a prophet, then who would be a teacher? If everyone were a doctor, then who would do the farming?

I have come to realize that although we were all created to be fruitful to the glory of the Lord, we are gifted to do it in different ways.

We are all created to let people know about God, to be reconciled to Him and enter His kingdom, but the way each person does it involves his or her gift. A pastor can preach in or out of the church and win souls to God, while a church member who happens to be a teacher, cashier or farmer can also be a great witness for Christ in the community and win souls to God.

Fortunately when we were born, we did not get to choose our gifts, talents or callings. We were created with those gifts. Later when we were born again, His purpose was already in us. It needs to be developed and used, but it's in there from the beginning. I will speak more about this in Chapter Six.

When it comes to developing your gifts, it is great for you to look up to people as mentors, but you cannot become them. You can glean from them, but you cannot be exactly who they are.

You cannot be someone else because you have to be you!

You were created to be you; you are wonderfully and fearfully (awesomely) made!

Just as you will never become someone else, someone else will never be you; there is only one of you, so be the "you" that you were created to be.

During a training program I attended, a classmate of mine came up with a great idea on how to teach a math topic—ratios—to young students in a fun way so they would understand the concept. She had the kids mix the colors in different proportions but to record what proportions they used in their combinations.

For example, if they wanted the secondary color green,

then they needed to record how many dabs of yellow paint and how many dabs of blue paint were used. 2 dabs of yellow and 1 dab of blue would be a ratio of 2:1. Other ratios could be 3:4, 1:3 and so on. At the end, the students ended up with different shades of green. No two shades of green were exactly the same.

Think about our God-given gifts in that sense; the incredible variety of combinations in all our genes and chromosomes is enough to boggle the mind.

Take, for example, one gift (my coveted gift of singing—you remember—the one that I didn't get!) This gift is very prominent; we have lots of people who are gifted to sing, but no two singers are exactly the same. No two singers have *exactly* the same style; they might be similar, but each of them has different backgrounds, experiences, tastes and personalities.

Each person's history gives him or her a unique story. We had several kings in the Bible—Saul, David, Solomon and so on. None of them had exactly the same history; they each had a unique story although they were all kings.

GIVE YOUR ALL

One story that helped me a great deal when it came to understanding the use of gifts is the story of the widow's two mites. Other stories like the parable of the talents convey a similar message, but the difference with this story is, less is more with God!

There was a widow who did not have much. She found herself in the midst of some wealthy individuals who were giving large amounts of money into the treasury. The widow only had two mites, but she was not going to let that deter her; she could not miss this opportunity to bless the LORD.

I suspect that she must have given in this way on a regular basis, however on this particular day Jesus noticed her. He said, *"...Assuredly, I say to you that this poor widow has put in more than all those who have given to the treasury; for they all put in out of their abundance, but she out of her poverty put in all that she had, her whole livelihood." (Mark 12:43-44)*

What she gave was worth more because she gave everything she had.

Her little was worth much more than the large sums the others offered. She gave God the best gift because she gave Him everything she had. Whatever your gift may be, you will not be judged by what measure you possess, but what measure you use. *To him to whom much is given, much is required. (Luke 12:48)*

I love numbers and I am often teased because I tend to think mathematically most times. When things are explained mathematically, I can easily relate. In this story, Jesus said the widow gave all she had— her whole livelihood. That means she gave one hundred percent. She had two mites and she gave both of them—two mites: (2 out of 2 is 2/2=100%). Let's say the others had about 100 mites and they gave twenty mites. Twenty is, of course, more than two, if you're just looking at numbers. However twenty out of a hundred is only twenty percent: (20 out of 100 = 20/100= 20%). This widow gave more than the others because she gave 100%. She gave all - everything!

So now the question is, how are you using your gifts? Are you giving all you have?

Remember how God has given to each of us a measure of faith? (Romans 12:3) To each member of the body, He has given a measure according to their function. One person's faith cannot be said to be greater than another's. They may exercise it in different ways, but they're each given that measure to work with.

Consider a pastor and a teacher. The pastor cannot be said to have more faith than the teacher.

Or consider a large ministry with thousands of members, compared to a small ministry with just a few members. The pastor of a 5,000-member church does not necessarily have more faith than the pastor of a 50-member church. (And after all, who can *measure* faith?)

God has given us these gifts through His grace so we can perform different functions at different levels, according to the measure of faith dealt to us. Only the Lord can decide whether it takes greater faith to run a smaller church than a larger church. And only the Lord can measure the impact either of those ministries might have; it's not always obvious to the eye or based on impressive numbers.

Remember in the beginning of this chapter when I was moaning about not being able to preach, dance or sing? Those would have been more highly visible gifts. But I had yet to discover how highly God values the hidden ones. God shows in His Scripture how precious they are:

> *And those members of the body which we think to be less honorable, on these we bestow greater honor; and our unpresentable parts have greater modesty, but our presentable parts have no need.* **But God composed the body, having given greater honor to that part which lacks it, that there should be no schism in the body, but that the members should have the same care for one another.** *And if one member suffers, all the members suffer with it; or if one member is honored, all*

44

*the members rejoice with it. (I Corinthians
12:23-26)*

You have a gift! While it might not be as prominent as
someone else's right now, let your goal in life be to use it
according to the measure of faith you have.

The question is not how much your measure is, but how
much you are using the measure you've been given. And
what is important is not that one's measure is greater than
another's, but that God is glorified (that He is first thanked)
in all, and also that there is no schism in the body. Give the
gift of yourself--that's one hundred percent (100%) of what
you have--to the Lord, just as the widow did, every day.

Growing up, whenever I prepared for a school exam, I
always aimed for an A or better; I figured that if I aimed for
the best, then I would do my best. If for some reason I fell
short, then I would still do well. This habit of mine was a
personal decision, not something I did to show off. In that
sense it was a hidden thing.

Later on when I was preparing for each exam in college,
I discovered that having this approach helped me excel.
As it turns out, God used that habit to help me excel in the
long run.

You too can adopt this attitude throughout your life.
**Aim to excel in whatever the Lord has called you to
do.** Let your goal be to use your gift in excellence; aim to do
your best and you will. Paul encourages us to run the race
to win a prize. (1 Corinthians 9:24-25)

Even if you don't win a visible prize as a result of your
efforts, your most valuable prize will be the way the Lord
works in your life as a result of you giving it your best.

When God gives you a gift, you may notice that the
enemy tries to distort it or create obstacles to discourage

you from using it. For example, someone who has a gift to encourage people might struggle with past hurts, timidity or rejection. Maybe those they try to encourage just use them and don't value them. That would shut them down pretty fast, wouldn't it?

Or maybe the encourager might try to help people who can't receive it; then they'd burn out and grow discouraged.

The enemy can also distort the gifts in the other direction; the encourager may feel they are superior to everyone else, thereby tearing them down instead of lifting them up. You may have seen examples of both kinds of situations in your life.

There are many ways these gifts can get derailed, interrupted or bent out of shape. Therefore make sure that you pursue healing in any area of your life where you've been hurt or rejected.

You'll find plenty of instances in the Bible were the enemy has interrupted people's gifts or tried to mess them up in some way. You saw in Chapter 2 how these things happened with both Moses and Jacob. Yet these men are just two of the many examples in the Scripture--people like you and me-- who experienced failure yet were still used in amazing ways.

DON'T BURY IT!
"Every good and perfect gift comes from the Father of Lights, in whom there is no variation or shadow of turning." (James 1:17)

Whatever gift God has given you is good; do not allow the enemy to discourage you from using your gift or cause you to use it perversely. Do not allow him convince you to that your gift is insignificant. The truth is, although these are considered gifts, we are held accountable for how we use them.

Take a look at the Parable of the Talents in Matthew

25:14: A man who was traveling to a far country gave talents (money) to three of his servants. After he returned, he asked for an account. Two servants, each given different amounts, had doubled what they were given. But the third one had buried his talent in the ground. He gained nothing and then ended up losing what he had. (Luke 19:11-27)

What a wasted opportunity that was!

In Luke 13, Jesus shares another parable, this time about a certain man who had a fig tree planted in his vineyard. For three years had sought for fruit but found none. We need to be accountable and fruitful with our gifts.

And it's not only about us; it's about being entrusted with something valuable from heaven. Jesus said that a man can receive nothing except it be given him from heaven. (John 3:27)

Every gift or talent we possess is from God; when we think of it this way, it helps us remain accountable and not bury this treasure that we're called to invest in the course of our lives.

Look at the Parable of the Good Samaritan (Luke 10:25-37) with this perspective of accountability in mind; imagine Jesus as the Good Samaritan and you as the innkeeper.

Just as the Samaritan brought the wounded man to the innkeeper, so Jesus brings wounded people into our lives for us to care for and nurture. He has also given us the provision (gifts and talents) to cover the expense of ministering to these wounded people. The Good Samaritan then says to the innkeeper, *"Take care of him; whatever more you spend, when I come I will repay." (v. 35)*

Notice the Samaritan did not expect the wounded man to take care of the payment. Nor did He expect the innkeeper to pay for the care himself. In the same way, God doesn't expect the wounded ones in our lives to be able to cover their expenses, nor does He expect us to minister to people on our own resources.

Sometimes when we have helped people, we tend to expect our reward from them. Maybe we don't expect payment in cash, but we might expect to be recognized or shown appreciation in some way. We might even go as far as feeling hurt or offended when we don't receive this kind of recognition.

I encourage you to not be offended when it seems as though you have been overlooked. After ministering to that need, if you are feeling unrewarded or overlooked in any way, lay that pain at the foot of the cross. Whatever expense you incurred while taking care of the broken people God has brought to you needs to be put on His tab.

Do not try to get your reward or praise from man; God will reward you in due time, when He revisits. Let us remember that if not for His grace or gift given to us, we would not be able to give or minister to that one. Realizing this helps us stay focused and encouraged till He comes back with our reward.

Jesus showed us what it truly means to be accountable. It's not just about reporting abstract figures to your boss. No, it's deeply personal and all about relationship.

Listen to what Jesus says as He's praying to the Father: *"While I was with them in the world, I kept them in Thy name. Those that Thou gavest Me I have kept, and none of them is lost, but the son of perdition, that the Scripture might be fulfilled."* (John 17:12, KJV)

He reminded the Father that of all that were given to Him, he lost none save Judas, that the Scripture might be fulfilled.

Why was this—the fact that He had lost none—important to Jesus?

Accountability!

It was all about His desire to honor the Father in all He did; He came to fulfill a certain purpose, and that purpose was not separate from His deep relationship with God the Father. All of God's resources were available to Jesus to help Him fulfill that purpose, and He didn't take that for granted.

So it is with us too.

Have you ever lost something that belonged to you? How did you feel about it?

How about losing something that belonged to another individual?

Is it safe for me to conclude that losing something that belongs to you might not hurt as much as losing something that belongs to someone else? The reality is this: For the average person, taking care of another individual's possession would elicit a greater sense of responsibility, given that the item wasn't theirs to lose.

Jesus asks us, *"If we have not been faithful in what is another man's, who will give us our own?"(Luke 16:12)* I believe that if we regard our gifts—talents, callings, friends—in the same way, we will be more deeply and personally accountable.

Many people feel as though they are lost because they have lost touch with their gifts and therefore they've lost their sense of purpose. That is how close the relationship is between our identity and our purpose.

I know this connection well, because I used to be one of those people. I can tell you now that my purpose has a lot to do with giving to others, lifting them up and encouraging them.

But for many years, I suffered rejection; I had been passed over so many times, and in the most obvious situations. It seemed as though the very ones I tried to give to were the ones who rejected me. I had poured my heart out for them and loved them, and then it seemed they forsook me and even held a grudge against me. (I don't share this to get sympathy, but I know that there may be some out there who are going through similar situations.)

For years I allowed the heartache to weigh me down. It got to a point where I built walls all around myself because I was tired of getting hurt.

Once someone expressed how they could see the pain in my eyes. How could that be? I had done all kinds of things in an effort to hide the pain and the ache, but to no avail; it was obvious.

What I didn't realize was this: The walls I'd built to protect myself also walled me off from exercising my own gifts, and from fully living out my purpose.

So the walls didn't actually help protect me from the pain because I still had the pain. You might say that was my way of burying my gift, like the servant who buried his talent.

We don't usually start out deciding to bury it; often it's a hurt or fear of getting hurt again that causes us to want to hide.

But then it's like burying *ourselves!*

It was only recently that I began to realize more about what I was going through. It was not about a personal rejection by those I had helped. They did not forsake me; it was simply time for them to move on. It was time for their next assignment and time for my next assignment. (Often God places certain people in our lives for a certain reason and season, and it's a disservice to both if one to tries to hold onto the old season.)

This realization made goodbyes a lot easier for me, and helped me heal from the old feelings of rejection. I learned that once we truly repent of our own self-protection and learn to trust Him, God redeems the time that we wasted on burying our gifts and refusing to step out. He healed the hurt and rejection I felt in the past. He also gave me more insight into how people feel when they have been shut down.

Having overcome in that area, I'm better equipped to help others who experience the same rejection. The main thing I had to do was look to God for comfort, wisdom and understanding.

If you've been hurt, built walls around yourself or buried your gifts, know that He is the one who can help tear down those walls, heal those hurts and help you to dust off your gifts and use them again.

You too can be better equipped after you have overcome. You will be able help people who the Lord has put in put in your path.

CHAPTER 5

Your Preparation... and Your Time

Therefore if anyone cleanses himself from the latter, he will be a vessel for honor, sanctified and useful for the Master, prepared for every good work. (2 Timothy 2:21)

"To everything there is a season, a time for every purpose under heaven." (Ecclesiastes 3:1)

"Is anything too hard for the LORD? At the appointed time I will return to you, according to the time of life, and Sarah shall have a son." (Genesis 18:14)

Everyone has to go through preparation.

And everyone has a time.

Preparation is a process. And a process takes time.

The word preparation comes from "prepare" which means to put in proper condition or readiness: Get ready!

Get ready for what?

Your time!

An expectant mother knows about getting ready. She knows that when her time comes, she is going to bring someone special into the world, and she begins to prepare for that child. Your purpose within you is just like that child. It is special and needs to be fulfilled at an appointed time.

What is the most common question asked of the expecting mother?

That's right: *"When are you due?"* It's understood that there is an appointed time for that baby to arrive.

When it comes to *your* appointed time to "arrive" and shine in your life, you may not be able to predict a specific due date. But you do have something in you that is designed to be birthed at the right time. And just as a wise mother does not wait for the time of delivery to prepare for her child, you ought not to wait till that time to prepare yourself.

When it comes to fulfillment of your purpose, both preparation and time come into play.

There are certain changes a mother must go through as she prepares for her child. Some of these just happen no matter what she does: Her body prepares by undergoing changes on every level—structural adjustments, respiratory and cardiovascular changes, skin changes and the like. (I'll go into these things in more detail in a later chapter, "Birthing Your Purpose.")

Other aspects of the preparation she can control: She can choose to take her vitamins, exercise and stay away from certain foods or substances that could harm the unborn child. She may also set up a nursery and gather clothes and supplies for her baby.

In the same way, **preparation for your purpose involves action on the part of both God and you**.

GOD'S PART AND YOUR PART

There are certain things God may take you through—things over which you may have no control—to prepare you for your purpose. This is what I mean by *process or experience.*

Then too, there are certain things you must take yourself through to prepare for your purpose: things such as prayer, Bible meditations & lessons, surrounding yourself with people who will challenge you and so on. We can refer to this as *training*; like an athlete must train through exercise to develop his muscles. (1 Timothy 4:8)

As for God's part, His preparation may come in different forms. He may work through your relationships, His anointing on your life, the experiences you go through, persecutions or trials you face. Have you realized that we have very little or no control over these things?

For instance, you cannot choose your biological parents or siblings. Also, to a degree you may be able to choose your friends but you cannot control who crosses your path in life. In fact if you take time to notice it, you'll find that He uses *everything* that happens to you.

Nothing is wasted.

However, preparation works hand-in-hand with time.

THE APPOINTED TIME

If you look through the stories of people in Scripture, you'll notice how each one had their time.

At the appointed time, God visited Abraham, and God told Abraham's wife Sarah (who thought she had missed her "time," given that she was past the age of childbearing) that she'd have a son. (Genesis 18:14)

At the appointed time, God visited Moses in the wilderness and charged him to lead Israel out of Egypt. (Acts 7:30)

Esther was brought into the palace, into a position of great influence, "for such a time as this." (Esther 4:14)

And at the appointed time, Peter changed careers to become a fisher of men. (Luke 5:10)

Jesus was about thirty years of age when he began his official ministry. (Luke 3:23) That was definitely his time.

This is not to say he did nothing for thirty years. I believe he was still about his "father's business," as he said when he was found in the temple at age 12, listening to the teachers and asking them questions. (Luke 2:49) And no doubt the time Jesus spent growing up in his family, obeying his mother, playing with his brothers and sisters and later helping Joseph with carpentry wasn't wasted either.

All of it contributed to his preparation for that three-year ministry season that changed the world.

Have you ever felt like you were on a long detour, trying to get to where you wanted to go but having to travel all these other roads first?

You may notice that many times, people in the Bible were called and even anointed for their purpose, then there was a long period before they actually got to do what God said they would do.

If you have ever felt that way, you can look to the Scriptures to see how those people handled that in-between "detour" time and find helpful encouragement there.

THE ANOINTING

How God anointed Jesus of Nazareth with the Holy Spirit and with power, who went about doing good and healing all who were oppressed by the devil, for God was with Him. (Acts 10:38)

When something or someone is anointed, it may mean that they've been "smeared" with oil... but spiritually, it means they've been consecrated, *set apart* for something. (Exodus 29:19-21)

Earmarked for a special purpose.

It may also mean they've been infused and empowered by God to do whatever they've been called to do.

We need God's anointing in our lives as we answer His call. We also need it every day. As we spend time in His presence, He will pour Himself into us.

Something happens when the anointing of God comes on your life. The effectiveness and fruitfulness in your life can be so much greater with the Spirit of God: *"...Not by might nor by power, but by My Spirit," says the Lord.* (Zechariah 4:6)

At the same time, being anointed doesn't mean that everything in your life will make sense or be laid out in a way that seems logical to you. Nor does it mean that you'll be a perfectly magnificent leader overnight.

David was anointed to be king when he was still just a shepherd boy, gifted with music. But as we have already seen, he didn't become king right away. That didn't happen until he was thirty. (2 Samuel 5:4)

However he'd already been in preparation as he watched his father's sheep. During that time he killed a lion and a bear with his bare hands to protect the sheep. He also played his harp and sang songs to God.

Later after David was anointed by Samuel, he was recommended to Saul the King to play for him and become his armor-bearer. Not yet king, but living in the king's palace: I believe that the whole time, David was being prepared for his kingship.

What amazes me is the recommendation that was given by one of Saul's servants for David. (Notice that God will put the right people in your life. Most of the time they are people He strategically places there to elevate you, and sometimes without your knowledge. People who, even if you were to choose, you would not be able to hand pick any finer.)

Here is the recommendation: "...skillful in playing, a mighty man of valor, a man of war, prudent in speech and a handsome person and the Lord is with him." (I Samuel 16:18)

What a great resume! And David had not yet killed Goliath the Giant.

I believe God's anointing made the difference. Though still a young shepherd, David had been anointed for *kingship*. Set apart for that special purpose. Perhaps he already carried within him some of the authority he'd later need as king.

NOTHING LIKE LIFE EXPERIENCE

While David was in the palace as Saul's armor-bearer and musician, how do you think God was getting him ready for his purpose? Just being in that setting would be a gold mine for an observer ready to learn.

David may have spent some of his time dreaming and thinking about different aspects of being a king. He may have seen things others outside the palace would not have seen.

Let us use our imaginations a little: While in the palace, David probably continued to pray and claim God's promises. He probably watched the king and how he handled certain situations.

As things took place in the kingdom, David got a close-up view of how Saul handled those things. You might think that whenever Saul was losing his temper or making unwise choices, he wasn't showing forth character that would be good preparation for David. But whether Saul handled things well or not, David still got to observe and learn. In all these situations, God still kept David covered.

If you are working for role models who don't have the best character, don't be dismayed. God can still use them to help you be prepared.

We know that David kept relying on God to show him what to do. And as you rely on God, He will show you what to do, too.

Many people find themselves in difficult job or ministry situations—they may have a boss who treats them unfairly, or co-workers who generally make their days miserable. They might want to gripe about those circumstances, avoid certain people or try to get a different job. It may be that changing jobs would solve some problems, but more often than not, the perfect training ground is that difficult situation. Is it fun? No. But it's good preparation nonetheless.

DON'T MISS THE LIFE LESSON

A friend of mine was frustrated with her job. She felt mistreated by her boss and a couple of her coworkers. She considered quitting her job or taking a sabbatical leave, but then she got a chance to attend a program that changed her thinking.

Later she shared her decision to stay at her job. A few months after that she was moved to a different position for which she had a different supervisor.

I went through something similar, however my situation ended differently. I did go ahead and quit my job for the same reasons. Let's just say it was an action I promised myself never to repeat. Not only did I lose a good job, but also it took a while before I got another one.

My grandmother gave me a good advice which I still remember to this day: She said, "The next time, before leaving a job, make sure you have already gotten another one" I was young, and—you guessed it—now I have become wiser.

One thing I have come to realize is that there are certain things we need to learn during difficult (sometimes frustrating) situations. If we decide to run away instead of facing them to gain the life lesson, then it is certain that we will repeat the process until that lesson is learned.

It's just like having to pass a test before moving to another level. Or going around the same mountain.

Are you going through a similar situation? Is this a tough season in your life?

Maybe it is not involving your job. It might be your ministry, your church, your family or a certain relationship.

STOP: Before you call it quits, spend some time seeking the Lord and wait (though it might be very difficult) till you hear what He wants you to do.

At times it could be tough to hear Him in the midst of the storm but be still. Don't panic or take hasty actions (easier said than done) and request lots of prayer. Sometimes God speaks *in* silence, and sometimes He speaks *with* silence. Trust God with the process!

STICKING IT OUT PRODUCES CHARACTER

And not only that, but we also glory in tribulations, knowing that tribulation produces perseverance; and perseverance, character; and character, hope. (Romans 5:3-4)

Back to David: Wasn't it beneficial to him that he did not quit or act rashly? Instead he behaved himself and acted with wisdom. Imagine what would have happened if David had thought to himself, "Samuel anointed me and said I'm supposed to be king, and King Saul doesn't know what he's doing! Besides, he's not obeying God all the time!" What if David had just bailed out?

Or imagine if he'd just decided to run ahead of God's timing and take over the kingdom. He had several opportunities to kill Saul, but refrained because it wasn't for him to do. Nor was it time for him to be king yet!

If David had either bailed out or taken over, he might possibly have still been king but he would have missed opportunities to be uniquely strengthened by God— opportunities that would only come when the going was difficult and required discernment that could only come from God.

Fortunately, David stuck it out; not only was he anointed but he also pressed in to develop a bigger vision that helped him hang in there for the long haul.

We know too that meanwhile, back at the palace, David was especially anointed to help calm Saul's nerves by playing his harp. The anointing helps you use your gifts effectively, and also aids in your promotion. At the same time trials, tribulations, and chastening from the Lord also help you to develop your character. (Hebrews 12:11)

It is wise to be mindful of the difference between gifts and character.

A person's gift can still be operating even when that person is out of fellowship with the Lord or making some really poor character choices.

You can see evidence of that happening with Saul; he could still prophesy even though many times he wasn't acting in obedience to the Lord.

And Samson still had his supernatural strength even when living a life of lust and disobedience. Facing a challenge in the midst of this lifestyle, Samson said, "I will go out as before, at other times, and shake myself free!" But he did not know that the Lord had departed from him. (Judges 16:20)

His strength was a gift and connected to a covenant God made with him, not because of his perfect walk or godly character. For the gifts and the calling of God are irrevocable. (Romans 11:29)

Therefore **do not conclude that someone's gifts or anointing are proof of closeness to God.**

We can see how David's gift of music plus the anointing on his life brought him before a king. While David waited for God's timing to become king, he didn't wait to use his gift. He developed it long before Samuel anointed him, by playing and singing in the field with his sheep.

It was the same with Joseph; he had to wait a couple of times—in the pit where his brothers threw him before selling him into slavery, then in prison in Egypt—but while enduring these apparent setbacks, he also kept using his gifts to serve others.

He too was young—only seventeen when he had his dream. (Genesis 37:2) He was thirty when he became second in command to Pharaoh. (Genesis 41:46) Then it would be many more years before his dream came to pass and he actually saw his brothers bowing down before him.

Did you ever consider that the setbacks that appear to be contrary to your purpose are the very ones that develop your integrity and help you grow stronger in the Lord?

When those detours and setbacks occur, one mistake we make stems from impatience or lack of vision. We try to jump ahead of what God is doing, and by doing that we cause ourselves needless pain.

Usually we don't jump ahead to intentionally snub God;

most of the time it's because we don't understand that we are still in God's process. We don't see the big picture.

But God knows that. He is so merciful and long-suffering and always has a way of working out those painful experiences and disappointments for our good, provided we remain in Him.

Remember this: **Your gift will bring you before kings and before greatness. Your gift will open doors for you—but you have to begin using it.**

It is wise to wait for God's timing and to trust that He will make a way, but it is not wise to wait to be brought before greatness before you begin using your gift.

Sometimes people feel they need to wait for that big promotion or glamorous opportunity to begin using their gifts. Do not wait! Begin using it now, so you will be well prepared when the time comes for you to shine.

THE TEN VIRGINS

The story of the ten virgins (Matthew 25:1-13) is a great example of being prepared—versus being unprepared—for your purpose. Recently the Lord gave me an insight into this story.

As the cry rang out at midnight that the bridegroom was coming, the ten virgins arose, trimmed their lamps and went out to meet him. But five of them, the foolish virgins, noticed that their lamps were starting to go out. The wise virgins had made sure to take extra oil to put in their lamps. The foolish virgins began to ask the wise ones for more oil.

"'No,' they replied. 'Lest there not be enough for us and you. Instead, go you rather to them that sell, and buy for yourselves.'"

There is a lot that can be derived from this story, however

the main point I would like to emphasize is the importance of preparation and timing in your life.

The virgins all had control over their lamps, but no control over the time the bridegroom would arrive.

How does this apply to you?

Like the wise virgins, you too can be prepared by taking care of your lamp.

Your true preparation is that time invested with God.

As we fellowship with the Lord, we receive additional oil in our vessels. Hallelujah!

The wise virgins had spent their own money on oil (yes there is a cost); their wicks were trimmed (your light shines brighter when you've allowed yourself to be 'trimmed back' by God); and they also made sure their vessels were *filled up* (as you are His vessel designed to be filled with His presence and move in the anointing of the Holy Spirit).

It takes time to invest yourself in fellowship with God.

It also takes time to receive what you need from God. No one else can do that for you.

When we spend time in His presence daily, praying and studying His word, we develop our relationship. The more time we spend with Him, the more we become like Him.

The reality is, as Christians we are in desperate need of the anointing of the Holy Spirit—received while spending time in God's Presence—in order to fulfill our purpose. As we go out there to minister (in whatever ministry we are called to), we make use of His anointing and we need to be refilled so as not to get burned out.

We need to be prepared at all times just like the wise ones were. We would be foolish if the opportunity or the appointed time came for us to enter into our purpose and we were not prepared. As the saying goes, 'Time waits for no one."

Many interpret this parable of the virgins as referring solely to the time when we are to "enter heaven" at the end of our lives. But Jesus is telling this parable about the *kingdom of heaven*, which Scripture says is *within you*, or *in your midst*. (Luke 17:21)

It's not only for later; it's about engaging in fullness of life starting *now*.

Several times in the Scriptures we see the phrases, "when the time came," "at the appointed time" and other like expressions. These show us the important role time plays in the fulfillment of our purpose.

Therefore it is expedient to not only "be in the right place, at the right time" but also to be prepared *all the time*.

ESTHER: A PICTURE OF PREPARATION
(For such a time as this)

Have you taken a look at Esther and how she prepared herself? Esther was an orphan and brought up by Mordecai her cousin. A young Jewish girl from a humble beginning who ended up as queen of Persia. She was the instrument God chose to interrupt the plan of the enemy, which was to annihilate all the Jews.

Esther was able to fulfill that purpose, not only because she was in the right place at the right time but because she was prepared.

She was originally brought in to King Ahasuerus to be part of a process to select a queen. This process would take a year of preparation: *"...six months with oil of myrrh, and six months with perfumes and preparations for beautifying women."* (Esther 2:12)

But Esther, a Jewess living in Persia, had very likely been

GO BE YOU TO THE FULLEST

prepared already and set apart in other ways, according to her people's traditions. Therefore when it was her turn to come into the king's chambers, there was something beyond her great beauty that stood out to him—and he made her queen.

Later, when Esther learned of the plot that had been devised by Haman to annihilate her people, she realized she was uniquely positioned to do something. But more preparation was needed.

She called for a three day fast, and she fasted herself; she wasn't going to act rashly or without teamwork.

Then before approaching the king, she *"put on her royal robes."* (Esther 5:1) (You may be reminded of how we are told not to trust in our own righteousness but to put on God's.)

No doubt Esther prayed as well, for unless the king extended his golden scepter, she would not live.

All this preparation for one meeting—yet what a powerful meeting it was! Esther effectively moved the heart of the king and saved the lives of all the Jews living in Persia at that time. **Her "time" was brief but her mission was huge.**

None of that preparation was wasted, and it was not merely about being beautiful; it was about genuine devotion to God, purity of heart and wisdom that depends on depth of character.

OUR BRIDAL PREPARATION

As the bride of Christ, we are being prepared to meet our King- the bridegroom Jesus Christ. This preparation is our life *process.*

We go through times of purification and times of beautification, just as Esther did. The blood of Jesus plays a huge role, as does the anointing of the Holy Spirit as we are in constant need of that purification and beautification.

The oil used in this process symbolizes the purifying qualities of the anointing in our lives. Myrrh, a symbol of death (one of the three gifts presented to the young child Jesus, signifying his suffering and death) is also used in this process. Myrrh comes from a dry resin (bitter tasting) extracted from certain tree species and can be used for perfume, incense, medicine...anointing or embalming.

The word myrrh comes from the Hebrew word "mor" which means bitter. (Wikipedia) As you go through life, pursuing your purpose, you will encounter bitter circumstances and may have to die to self, many times. But do not allow these things to hinder you.

"Then He said to them all, 'If anyone desires to come after Me, let him deny himself, and take up his cross daily, and follow Me.'" (Luke 9:23) As Christians we are invited to take up this cross and die daily. Paul is a great example of this: *"I assure you, believers, by the pride which I have in you in [your union with] Christ Jesus our Lord, I die daily [I face death and die to self]." (1Corinthians 15:23, AMP)*

Some of us brethren face death literally every day, such as those Christians who are being persecuted in different parts of the world.

As for dying to self, it is inevitable but necessary, to bring us into greater life. What a paradox! The process you are going through may be painful and bitter, but you will reap the benefits, if you stay in Him.

You will find all kinds of examples of preparation in the Bible; hardly anyone was exempt from having to go through some kind of time being set apart to get ready:

- The Israelites were being *prepared* as they journeyed through the wilderness so as not to faint in *time* of war.
- Jesus was led by the Spirit to the wilderness and was there forty days and nights, after which his ministry began.
- Moses was prepared in the wilderness before being sent to present himself to Pharaoh and request the release of God's people.
- Esther is only one of many, and she does shine as an excellent example of one who did not rush into things, nor did she hold back when it was time to step in. Her timing was a perfect picture for us, of how to respond to God in our process.

Often people make the mistake of thinking that their ministry will begin only after they are married—so they put everything on hold. If Esther had waited for marriage to take her time with God seriously, she might not have had such a head on her shoulders when the time came.

Before I was married, I received some good advice: "Begin to prepare yourself *before* you meet your spouse, so that when the time comes, you are a helpmeet and not a burden to him."

There are things you may not be able to do after marriage, so take the time now to begin achieving them. While you wait to meet that special one, equip yourself—get an education, train yourself, get a job, pursue your own adventures in the Lord. Then when you meet your spouse, you will be better prepared to bless him or her and not be a burden. Another advantage to this is that you will be so well occupied that you won't feel as though it's taking too long.

TREE TENDING

Even a plant has to be prepared to bear fruit. In many cases pruning is required in order to produce more fruit. When a tree is pruned, the cutting might seem drastic, like it's being killed.

Dead wood has to be cut away, but also even healthy branches need to be cut back to help the tree become healthier. There are some things—even some relationships in our lives—that need to be broken off because they are dead wood, not fruitful. Needless to say, the pruning process does not feel good.

Did you ever hear some people complain about God's process in their lives? Maybe you've been one of them—crying out, "Lord, you're killing me here!"

Or have you ever felt like you were being crushed?

Sometimes it may feel like that. *"We are hard-pressed on every side, yet not crushed; we are perplexed, but not in despair; persecuted, but not forsaken; struck down, but not destroyed."* (2 Corinthians 4: 8-9)

But it's for a good purpose. It's for your growth and preparation.

Check out the story in Luke 13 about the barren fig tree. The owner comes to seek fruit, but there is none, so he orders it to be cut down. However the keeper asks for a year to dig around and fertilize it first—that is, to prepare it.

You will notice that he had to add some things (fertilizer) and he had to rearrange or take away some things (dig around its base). Either way, much of the preparation is about receiving care. It's not all up to the fig tree; it's also up to the one tending it.

I believe the owner of the fig tree is our Lord; we are the tree, and the keeper is the Holy Spirit. You may have noticed how the Holy Spirit works in our lives to enable us to bear fruit—richer fruit.

He digs around the foundation of our lives to remove filth like sin, unforgiveness, bitterness and anything that would hinder us from growing.

And He fertilizes us by releasing His gifts and nurture for our spirits.

The fruit we see will be the fruit of the Spirit—love, joy, peace, patience, kindness, goodness, self-control—and it will also be a transformed life that will transform other lives.

As mentioned before, much of your preparation may involve time spent receiving from the Lord.

The Holy Spirit will do His part, but we have to do ours: Abide in Him!

You abide in Him by spending time with Him through prayer and meditation and immersing yourself in His word. Yes, you can expect some pruning and some upheaval during that time, but it's worth it for the extra life springing up through you!

When the Lord comes seeking fruit in your life, will you be ready? Will you be prepared, or will you require more time?

I struggled for a long time in my life thinking, "If I just do what's right—if I cross all my t's and dot all my i's—if I do what's right and never do what's wrong—then just maybe the Lord will use me mightily."

But that makes everything depend on me! That's a system based on my performance, not on abiding in the Lord.

Later I realized that God had a time for me; that all He required of me was to stay faithful and not depend on my righteousness. Besides, my own righteousness is "as filthy rags" before Him anyway! He showed me I was to depend on His righteousness. And as I look back over my life, I see how different experiences, good or bad, right or wrong,

YOUR PREPARATION...AND YOUR TIME

tender or painful, convenient or not... (including those I personally wouldn't have chosen to go through), all worked out to prepare me for my purpose, my call and my time in ministry.

WAIT FOR IT

*"Then the LORD answered me and said: 'Write the vision and make it plain on tablets, that he may run who reads it. For the vision is yet for **an appointed time**; but at the end it will speak, and it will not lie. Though it tarries, wait for it; because it will surely come, it will not tarry.'"* (Habakkuk 2:2-3)

God is all knowing—omniscient—and therefore knows the specific date an event will occur. However we humans are limited in our knowledge. As a result, often it seems as though God is taking a loooong time to fulfill a promise He has made.

Look at instances like Abraham waiting for his promised heir; Isaac arrived when Abraham was one hundred years old. (Genesis 21:5)

The Israelites' deliverance came after their sojourn of four hundred and thirty years. (Exodus 12:40-41)

Daniel sought the Lord after he understood the number of years specified; seventy years had to be accomplished first. (Daniel 9:2-3)

The point I am trying to make is that we are limited in our flesh when it comes to understanding God's timing and therefore we become frantic when we do not see what has been promised to us. God's timing is not necessarily about a specific date on the calendar. It has more to do with one event succeeding another, hence the phrases like, *an appointed time, a set time...*

70

Those dreams or visions the Lord has given you, the prophecies His ministers have confirmed, the signs He showed you are all for an appointed time.

The promise of the Messiah, though prophesied hundreds of years earlier, came to pass at the appointed time. (Galatians 4:4) Besides, with the Lord, one day is as a thousand years and a thousand years is as a day! (2 Peter 3:8)

Wait for God's time, and while waiting, like Daniel—be prayerful; like Joseph—be faithful; like Ruth—be committed; like Mary—be obedient; like David—behave wisely; and like Moses, be humble.

The dream or purpose may seem delayed but it will not be denied. As the songwriter perfectly puts it, He is an on time God, He may not come when you want Him but He'll be there right on time. Be encouraged; God knows exactly what He is doing.

While there are things we can do, it doesn't mean we are to do everything on our own strength. Wait on Him and in Him, for God's promises in Him are yes and in Him Amen!

Don't allow yourself to stray, but if you do find yourself far away, turn around and come back to Him, for He is faithful and He will never fail. Stay in Him, and at the right time, He will bring that dream to pass; His purpose in your life will be fulfilled in due season.

*In the Lord I need to **stay***
*Never allow myself to **stray***
*And if I find myself **away***
*I will get on my knees and **pray***
*For my sins, he died to **pay***
*To give me hope each and every **day**!*
(Ayileru Morton)

CHAPTER 6

Your will, God's will

"Not everyone who says to Me, 'Lord, Lord,' shall enter the kingdom of heaven, but he who does the will of My Father in heaven." (Matthew 7:21)

"For I have come down from heaven, not to do My own will, but the will of Him who sent Me. This is the will of the Father who sent Me, that of all He has given Me I should lose nothing, but should raise it up at the last day. And this is the will of Him who sent Me, that everyone who sees the Son and believes in Him may have everlasting life; and I will raise him up at the last day." (John 6:38-40)

"Your kingdom come. Your will be done. On earth as it is in heaven." (Matthew 6:10)

Everyone has a free will...to choose God's will

"Therefore, as the Holy Spirit says: 'Today, if you will hear His voice, do not harden your hearts as in the rebellion ....'" (Hebrews 3:7 & 8)

"And if it seems evil to you to serve the Lord, choose for yourselves this day whom you will serve, whether the gods which your fathers served that were on the other side of the River, or the gods of the Amorites, in whose land you

dwell. But as for me and my house, we will serve the Lord." *(Joshua 24:15)*

Do you want to know God's will for your life?

Some people have the wrong idea; they might say they "just want to do God's will," but meanwhile they want to preach like someone else, they want to dance like someone else, and they want to sing like someone else. But that may not be God's will for them. This is their thinking: *If I look this way, if I act like someone who goes to church, if I fast like this person or pray like that person, then maybe I will make it in.*

Jesus says in Matthew 7:21 that not everyone who calls Him Lord will enter the kingdom of heaven but he who ***does the will of his Father*** in heaven. Furthermore Jesus explains, even those who claim to have prophesied or cast out demons will not be spared. Through this we realize the importance of doing God's will; it is not about the gifts or talents you possess; it is not even about doing all sorts of miracles; it is about God's will. Our Lord's Prayer contains these words, "...***Your will be done*** *on earth as it is in heaven."* Once again we see how significant God's will is in our lives, here and beyond.

God has a will for your life as well as a will for the lives of others.

God's will for you is to fulfill His purpose for your life. And He gave you a will to freely choose to follow His will.

GOD'S OVERALL WILL

"For this is good and acceptable in the sight of God our Savior, who desires all men to be saved and to come to the knowledge of the truth." (1Timothy 2:3 & 4)

*The Lord is not slack concerning His promise, as some count slackness, but is longsuffering toward us, **not willing** that any should perish but that all should come to repentance. (2 Peter 3:9)*

"Go therefore and make disciples of all the nations, baptizing them in the name of the Father and of the Son and of the Holy Spirit, teaching them to observe all things that I have commanded you; and lo, I am with you always, even to the end of the age." Amen. (Matthew 28:19 & 20)

God's will is that no one should perish but all should repent. And Jesus commands us to go make disciples. From these Scriptures and many more, I would conclude that God's will for us is to tell others about Him and bring people to Him so that no one perishes.

I believe that this is God's ultimate will for our lives. He does not want any to perish. He wants all to come to the knowledge of the truth. So whatever gifts, talents, grace, and callings we are given are for one purpose – to be fruitful in His kingdom and shine in such a manner that helps someone see God.

In this way, God has chosen to need us. Imagine that!

Because God has given us free will, He's chosen to make Himself open to us and to the choices we make. All the more reason to honor Him by aligning with His will.

There is no greater example of alignment with this ultimate will than our Lord Jesus.

He was born to die, to redeem us; that was God's will for His life. Over and over again we see the prophecies in Scripture that predicted his birth, life and death. There was a time for His suffering and death to be accomplished, however before that time came Jesus was busy teaching, preaching, working miracles. When the time came, He went in obedience, even to death. (Philippians 2:8)

The Bible says He suffered. *Though He was a Son, yet He learned obedience by the things which He suffered. (Hebrews 5:8)* His suffering taught Him obedience. He was never disobedient, however. He went through suffering, and the suffering He went through taught Him how to obey.

The word of God also tells us that tribulations work out patience; and patience, experience; and experience, hope. (Romans 5: 3-4)

Everything He went through was to bring people to repentance, for advancement in God's kingdom. (John 6:38)

Everything He did was a fulfillment of God's plan. He conformed His life to the Lord's Prayer: *"Thy will be done on earth as it is in heaven." (Matthew 6:10)*

While walking through this earth, it is good for us to be focused on doing God's will. Jesus was so focused on the will of God that He referred to it as food and drink. When he had a meeting with the woman at the well, His disciples invited Him to eat, having no clue what was happening in the realm of the Spirit.

His response to them was, *"I have food to eat of which you do not know."* And later, **"My food is to do the will of Him who sent me, and to finish His work." (John 4:34)**

God's will does not always come easy. Sometimes there is a struggle to do His will. When there is a struggle, it may help us to remember that He always works it out for good. (Romans 8:28)

JESUS' STRUGGLE IN THE GARDEN

There will be some moments in our lives when we will be faced with decisions to accept and carry out God's will; these moments might not be the easiest of situations. However if we say yes to Him, at the end of the day we will come out victorious.

When it was time for Jesus to go to the cross, He was faced with possibly the most difficult decision on earth. We see him in the Garden of Gethsemane, praying with His sweat pouring out like great drops of blood – (can you say *struggle?*) – because He knew the extent of what He was about to go through.

Before His crucifixion, Jesus prayed, *"O My Father, if it is possible, let this cup pass from me; nevertheless, not as I will, but as **You will**." (Matthew 26:39)*

He was already betrayed and rejected by the very ones (meaning humanity) that He came to save; He was about to be crucified—the kind of death reserved for a common criminal. The one who knew no sin was about to be imputed with the sin of the whole world. And if that weren't enough, His Father would forsake Him.

Have you ever been through a situation or trial in which you had absolutely no one to turn to? Did you ever feel totally alone because everyone seemed to have forsaken you?

You are not alone! Jesus is with you and He knows exactly how you feel. (Hebrews 4:15) Let's take a closer look at the process he went through:

"O My Father, if it is possible, let this cup pass from me; nevertheless, not as I will, but as You will..."

"O My Father, if this cup cannot pass away from me unless I drink it, Your will be done." (Matthew 26:39, 42)

Although Jesus cried that the cup would pass, His earnest desire was that God's will would be accomplished.

"Shall I not drink the cup which My Father has given Me?" (John 18:11)

Jesus, knowing that all things were now accomplished, that the Scripture might be fulfilled, said, "I thirst!" (John 19:28)

In the last verse above, we see that Jesus cries out, "I thirst!"

For a long time I pondered on this particular verse. Although there are various explanations, I believe it was deeper than a physical thirst.

One morning, after spending the night at my in-laws, I was in the basement trying to have my quiet time and suddenly there it was. I spotted a picture that had probably been there for a while, but I'd never taken notice of it before. No doubt I'd seen it in the past because I had been down there on several occasions, but this time it was different.

The picture showed the face of Jesus. He was wearing a crown of thorns and it had the inscription, "I thirst." Suddenly it hit me. At that moment it was as though scales fell off my eyes and I saw it clearly for the very first time. This is what I received:

As we saw in earlier passages, Jesus often referred to God's will as food and drink. In the garden of Gethsemane, Jesus prayed that the cup would pass, yet afterwards He accepted the cup—God's will.

When Judas came to get Him with the soldiers, Peter cut off the right ear of one of the soldiers, which Jesus promptly healed. Jesus asked Peter, "Shall I not drink the cup which My Father has given Me?" After which He was taken away for trial and then to the cross.

While He hung on the cross, He cried out, "I thirst!"

What was Jesus thirsty for? A drink?

I do not think so! Of course it was excruciating to be crucified, but I believe He was way beyond physical need at that point.

Jesus was thirsty for God's *will*; He had cried earlier for it to pass and then He had accepted it.

At this moment Jesus had gotten to the point where He was longing, desirous, yearning, hungry and yes, thirsty for God's will to be done. (Psalm 42:1) His earnest desire became God's desire.

GOD'S DESIRE, YOUR DESIRE

Are you faced with a difficult situation in your life right now?

Are you faced with a decision to make and you know what God says to do but it seems too difficult?

Your desire is to do God's will, but you need the strength to carry it out?

My advice is for you to spend some time tarrying in His presence like Jesus did at the garden of Gethsemane.

On the other hand, you might not know God's will for your current situation. The best thing to do is begin praying for revelation of His will. It could be made clear through your desire, or the best way He knows (a way you may not understand at the time).

When I'm in that place, I pray this way: "Lord reveal your will to me through my desire."

If I am still uncertain, I pray this way: "Lord, let your will be done."

It is best for us to follow the example of Christ; as we observe Him always conscious of—and always striving to do—the will of the Father throughout his entire life. As Jesus went before us and submitted Himself fully to the Father's will, we are empowered to offer ourselves in the same way. The Apostle Paul says it well in Romans:

"I beseech you therefore, brethren, by the mercies of God, that you present your bodies a living sacrifice, holy, acceptable to God, which is your reasonable service. And do not be conformed to this world, but be transformed by the renewing of your minds, that you may prove what is

that good and acceptable and perfect will of God." (Romans 12:1-2)

THOSE WHO'VE GONE BEFORE US

There are others in the Bible whose priority in life was to fulfill God's will.

John the Baptist is a great example—he was born to reveal Jesus. (John 1:31, Matthew 3:15)

Another great example is Deborah the prophetess who judged Israel. Deborah told Barak the Lord had commanded him to prepare for war—that He would deploy Sisera against him and give him (Barak) victory. (Judges 4:6-8) However, Barak refused to go unless she agreed to go with him. Determined that God's will be done, Deborah agreed to go with him, but told him of the consequence: the Lord would sell Sisera into the hand of a woman.

Has the Lord instructed you to do something or revealed a certain need which He wants you to fulfill? Is it challenging you out of your comfort zone?

Do not be discouraged or allow fear paralyze you. It's God's way of developing your reliance on Him.

Paul said he would rather boast in his weakness that the power of Christ would rest upon him. When he was weak then the he was strong because of his reliance on God's strength. (2 Corinthians 12:9-10)

Therefore when you encounter those situations, do not shy away or quit! Be courageous...take a step of faith.

Do you recall Rahab? She was not so pure (who is?) but she saw a need and acted by faith. (Hebrews 11:31) She took a risk when she hid the spies Joshua sent to Jericho. However in the end she reaped great benefits for herself and her whole family. (Joshua 6:25)

Imagine what would have happened if Rahab had not acted because of fear. Or if Esther had not stepped out when she needed to go before the king. They both took risks for the Lord, and both were greatly rewarded.

"Trust in the Lord with all your heart, and lean not on your own understanding." (Proverbs 3:5)

MANY ARE CALLED...

There have been a few times when I've been approached to respond to a challenging need. I had to think and pray about it.

What if I fail...? I thought...

(But what if I succeed?)

I felt inadequate. I felt as though I couldn't do it—I couldn't accomplish this task. I was afraid of failing, but then when I thought about it, I realized that was all the more reason to trust God and wholly depend on Him.

Then if *that* didn't get me moving, this thought did:

If I refuse to fill in where He needs me, I will miss out on my reward!

What an honor and a blessing in itself when God calls on us! If we say no, He can (and does) call on others. *"For many are called, but few are chosen."* (Matthew 22:14)

I used to view this verse a certain way. I thought it meant that the Lord called many and only chose a few (kind of like an exclusive club) ...until one day I got a revelation.

It was an eye opener!

You see, the Lord calls many, but as we noticed, only a few answer His call.

The few who respond to His call are the chosen.

Not everyone is willing to do His will, or to go through the preparation process we've been describing in this book.

That's why it is only a few who are chosen. They self-select by their willingness to accept His will.

It's worth noting that while God loves us unconditionally whether we say yes or no to his will, that doesn't mean everything will be easy for us all the time. "In this world, you will have tribulation. But take courage! I have overcome the world." (John 16:33)

Nor does it mean He will overlook our wrong choices, attitudes and actions. All our actions tend to have built-in consequences. In everything we do, we are either moving along with God's will, or going against His will. If we are not aligning ourselves with Him, then we are fighting against Him. (Matthew 12:30)

As you will see in Scripture, God will go the extra mile to work with us anyway, to get through to us and redeem the situation. But in those cases you can't expect to "have it *your* way...."

RUNNING CONTRARY?

Fighting against God's will can be very costly. Let us take the story of Balaam as an example. Initially he was told not to go with Balak's messengers and not to curse Israel, for they were blessed. But Balaam was disobedient, and he would have been killed if not for his donkey.

After Balaam's eyes were opened, the angel of the Lord said to him, *"I have come out to stand against you because your way is perverse before Me." (Numbers 22:32)*

Balaam was not following the will of God because his way was perverse; as a result God was against him.

Another example is Jonah, who tried to run away from God's will by getting into a boat going in the opposite direction.

God sent a great wind, but Jonah was asleep until the captain found him. The crew finally discerned that he'd fled from the presence of God.

Reluctantly, at Jonah's request the men threw him into the sea, where a great fish swallowed him. In the belly of the fish, Jonah repented and accepted God's will. God spoke to the fish and it vomited him out. (Jonah 1 & 2)

Are you running away from God's will for your life?

If so you are going against Him, just like Paul who kicked against the goads. (Acts 9:3-6)

It is not possible to be both against Him and with Him, so turn around and get back in line with His will.

The Bible makes it very clear that there are consequences for refusing to yield to God's will. There are also benefits that come with abiding in God's will. (I John 5:14)

We ought not to wrestle *against* the Lord or His will; what we need to wrestle *against* are principalities, powers, spiritual wickedness. (Ephesians 6:12)

At times we run away from doing God's will because we are afraid of the cost; we worry about what we will have to give up. The truth is that it is actually more costly to go against his will.

We think we cannot afford to surrender, when in fact we cannot afford *not to*.

If we choose to do His will, all we have to lose is pride. Good riddance! Look at it this way: At the end of the day, it is the fear of being broken that causes us to run. However, being broken *in* His will is far more fruitful than being broken *outside* of His will. Ask Jacob...

JACOB

God appeared to Jacob in a dream, told him to return to the land of his family, and he was obedient. He took his belongings and he stole away, leaving without saying goodbye.

Sometimes when God has asked us to leave, stopping to say goodbye entangles us again. When a new disciple of Jesus wanted to bid farewell to those at his house, Jesus said to him, *"No one, having put his hand to the plow, and looking back, is fit for the kingdom of God." (Luke 9:62)*

When God tells you to move, it is expedient that you move. Do not look back like Lot's wife. (Gen 19:26)

Do not tarry, and do not allow fear stop you or freeze you in your tracks. You may not understand why at the time, but you need to be obedient even if you have to move in fear, as Gideon did. (Judges 6:27)

So Jacob may have been afraid, which may explain why he left while Laban was out.

After Jacob left, his uncle found out he was gone and came after him. But even then, God warned Jacob in a dream not to say anything good or bad to Laban. God was with him because he was acting in obedience to His will.

Fast forward: The messengers Jacob had sent to his brother came back with some news. Esau was coming to meet him with four hundred men. Needless to say, Jacob was greatly afraid. He sent gifts ahead, trying as usual to work his way out with his schemes. Then he reminded God of His promise, sent the members of his camp and all his possessions over the brook, and got alone with God.

That night Jacob wrestled with a Man (an "angel of the Lord") until the break of day, and would not let Him go until he got his blessing:

"Your name shall no longer be called Jacob, but Israel;

for you have struggled with God and with men, and have prevailed." (Genesis 32:28)

WRESTLING WITH GOD

Why was Jacob able to wrestle with God and prevail? Was he stronger than the Lord?

Notice the Bible says he wrestled *with*, not *against*, the Lord.

I believe that the reason he prevailed was that He was in God's will. Jacob was told to return and he obeyed God; therefore he was not in opposition to God's will.

Of course he was not perfect, but at the very least, he was struggling *toward* God, not away from Him. This is the reason he could wrestle with the Lord and not against him. In contrast, when we are bent in disobedience to God's will, then we find ourselves wrestling against God.

PREVAILING WITH A GOOD FATHER

Often my husband plays with the kids and wrestles with them for fun—they are boys and crave this hands-on Daddy time. Still, when they wrestle, I fear for their safety because he is more powerful than they are. He tries to calm my nerves by saying, "Do you think I would ever hurt them? They are my kids!"

As they wrestle, he allows them to prevail. Why? Because they are his children and he has a healthy relationship with them.

If he were in a real wrestling match with someone, that would not be the case; he would make sure he emerged the winner. But his kids have the privilege of emerging the winner when they wrestle with their father. It is the same with God's kids.

So it was with Jacob; he prevailed in this wrestling match with God. That was not the case with Balaam or Jonah.

Jacob was doing exactly what God told him to do, therefore he wrestled with the Lord and not against Him; he prevailed—was broken in the process but got his blessing and his life is changed forever. (Genesis 32:22-30)

As I reflect on this experience of Jacob, I am reminded of this verse: *"And whoever falls on this stone will be broken; but on whomever it falls, it will grind him to powder."* *(Matthew 21:44)*

My husband allows the children to fall on him all the time. They might hurt a little—but what if he fell on them? The results would be crushing. Jacob was broken from this experience because he fell on the rock when he wrestled with God. However if the rock had fallen on him (if he had been wrestling *against* God), he would have been ground into powder.

Are you in God's will? Are you wrestling with God or against Him?

In God's will we are safe. Yes, we might be broken, but we remain blessed because God does not despise a broken heart (Psalm 51:17) but rather He is near to those who have a broken heart. (Psalm 34:18) He's chosen to make Himself open and available to you.

In fact, God has chosen to *need* you! Will you choose to make yourself available to Him?

GOD'S SPECIFIC NEED FOR YOU

In a marketing class I took, we broke into groups and were given an assignment to come up with a breakthrough innovation—something that had never been invented before. Our teacher advised us that the best way to start was to first search for a need.

We all acknowledged that there had been plenty of times in our lives when we thought it would be great if a certain product existed that could perform a given task. However in this case, we were stumped and could not come up with a need.

Have you ever been in a situation where you have been put on the spot? Say, someone asks you to suggest a song, and every song you like suddenly disappears from your mind? I don't know if it was a mental lapse or brain cramp—but we went blank at that moment. A whole team of six students could not come up with a genuine need, much less a product that we wished existed!

Why do I share that experience? To drive home this point: **A need has to exist before something is created.** In order to invent or create a product that would sell or become a breakthrough invention, we had to begin with a need. If there were no need or use for this product, then there would be no demand for it. No one would want to purchase it because they would have no use for it.

Whoever invented the telephone saw the need for people to communicate without having to leave their homes; whoever invented the microwave knew people were busy and hungry and wanted their food fast.

This is also how it is in heaven; the need for YOU existed before God made you. You are a breakthrough invention!

The Lord saw a need and then created YOU with that need in mind. God did not create you only to wait to see where you would fit in or what purpose you would fulfill. The need for you already existed; you are needed, you are useful, and there is a place for you.

Now for you theologians out there, yes I know that God is self-sufficient and in fact "needs" nothing. Our language cannot describe God's attributes adequately, and certainly not using the word "need." But look at how He looks to humanity for help:

Also I heard the voice of the Lord, saying, "Whom shall I send, and who will go for Us?"

Then I said, "Here am I! Send me." (Isaiah 6:8)

There are many other examples of this kind of seeking and sending. You can see from Scripture that God has chosen to need us. The Bible is full of His longing for us, not to mention countless stories about those He has asked to help Him. God set things up in such a way that there's an opening for each of us to partner with Him.

"Your eyes saw my substance, being yet unformed.

And in Your book they all were written,

The days fashioned for me,

When as yet there were none of them." (Psalm 139:16)

The above Scripture is one of the instances in the Bible where the Lord shows us that His plan for us existed before we were born. And if He planned for us, He's established a need for us.

"Before I formed you in the womb I knew you;

Before you were born I sanctified you;

I ordained you a prophet to the nations." (Jeremiah 1:5)

The Lord revealed this to Jeremiah when he was called. God's thoughts towards us are thoughts of peace and not of evil, to give us a future and a hope. (Jeremiah 29:11) God knew you before you were born, while in your mother's womb. Also He knew you before you responded to His call as Christian. His plans for us reveal the position He called us to fill.

"And we know that all things work together for good to

those who love God, to those who are the called according to His purpose. For whom He foreknew, He also predestined to be conformed to the image of His Son, that He might be the firstborn among many brethren. Moreover whom He predestined, these He also called." (Romans 8:28-30)

CALLED ACCORDING TO HIS PURPOSE

When God called you, He willed you into existence, and you were given a free will to choose to love him and respond to His call.

I started this chapter by stating that a need exists before a product is invented. Let's visit Romans 8:28 to shed more light on this.

The Bible says that we are "the called" according to his purpose. As a child of God, the Lord's purpose, plan, thought, will and desire for you existed before you became a Christian. (Psalm 139) We can conclude from this that God's need for you and His purpose existed, and then you were created, born, called to fulfill it.

JOSIAH

The story of King Josiah is another great example of God answering a need with a person. In 1 Kings 13, the people of Israel were led by an evil king and had strayed away from God to serve other gods. Their ways were evil before God, so He sent a young prophet to prophesy of a coming king named Josiah who would restore order to Israel.

In 2 Kings 22, we see that prophecy coming to pass—a young boy named Josiah becomes king of Israel at the age of eight. God saw the need for Josiah before he was born, and when he was born, he fulfilled that need.

MARY

Throughout the Old Testament we see prophecies about the birth of the Savior. Not only was His birth foretold, but also the human vessel that God would use to fulfill this need was announced in Isaiah 7:14 as a sign: A virgin would bring forth a son and would call his name Immanuel.

In Matthew 1, Mary was chosen as the vessel that would be with child and give birth to Jesus. She submitted to God's will (Luke 1:38) and brought forth a Son. God saw the need for Mary before she was born, and many years later she fulfilled that need.

SOLOMON

In 1 Chronicles 17, God sends Nathan the prophet to inform David that he would not build the house of God but that his seed—one of his sons—would be the one to build God's house. In 2 Chronicles 5, Solomon builds the temple and dedicates it to God after completion. God had a need for Solomon before he was born, and he fulfilled that need.

These are only a few examples in which God foresaw a need and revealed to people how He had already made provision for that need to be met.

Lastly I would not do justice to this topic if I did not include this wonderful story of God's strategic provision.

THE LORD HAS NEED OF THEE

And if anyone says anything to you, you shall say, 'The Lord has need of them,' and immediately he will send them." *(Matthew 21:3)*

One day I heard so clearly in my heart, "The Lord has need of you."

Most of us have heard the story about the triumphal entry. The Lord sent his disciples to get a colt for his entry into Jerusalem. He directed them to a specific place to loose the colt, and instructed them on what answer to give in the event they were interrogated. He said, "Say to them, 'The Lord has need of it.'"

This story can be viewed from other perspectives, but here I'm focusing on the perspective of the need. That colt was there for a reason and for a season; when it was time and the need arose, the colt was useful.

Let's get in the colt's mind for a little bit: If the colt could talk, he probably had questions while waiting:

When will I be used? Why am I here?

Am I going to get to do anything?

Am I not good enough?

Maybe the colt was belittled occasionally, or looked on with disdain. He had never been sat on or ridden.

It's interesting that while a colt is defined as a young male horse [or donkey] of not more than four years old, another source (dictionary.com) defines a colt as a young or inexperienced *person*.

I find it amazing and wonderful how Jesus used something that was young and inexperienced in the eyes of others.

Sometimes people may view you as being inexperienced (just like they viewed David, as we saw in previous chapters). But the Lord knows who you are and what He has taken you through. Although God guides you through situations to help build your experience, He is still able to use those who are inexperienced because of what He has already placed in them.

Do not be discouraged because you lack experience in a

certain area. Trust God and move according to His leading. He is able to make up the difference. Don't be concerned with whatever you lack when you act in obedience.

If the Lord can use a colt, He can certainly use you.

God is able to add Himself to your willingness, and in turn, you get to share in the honor of carrying Him.

Can the Lord ride on you? Will you make yourself available to Him?

The Lord has need of you! You are useful and have a special role to play!

CHAPTER 7

Discovering Your Purpose

For a long time I made efforts to find out what my gifts and callings were. Many times as a young child, I was asked what I wanted to do or become in life... but I had no answers.

Then as a young Christian, I was faced with the same dilemma; people would ask me what my ministry was.

What was I called to do?

I realized that although I had an idea of what I saw myself doing, I had a difficult time describing it to someone else.

Fast forward to my life as an adult: As a pastor's wife, at first I felt I needed to be a choir director, a praise and worship leader or a music minister or something of that sort. I believed that was the expectation for pastors' wives even though I was none of the above.

Furthermore I realized I did not have a gift for preaching, nor was I well fitted to be a worship leader...(the list could go on). Therefore my search began!

At that point I cried out to God because (as I said earlier) I was convinced that I had no callings or gifts. It was then that certain scriptures came into my heart—verses like, *"God is no respecter of persons" (Acts 10:34 KJV)* and *"God has dealt to each one a measure of faith." (Romans 12:3)*

I was encouraged.

I still didn't know what I was supposed to do, but at least I had some hope at that point.

What then was my calling, purpose, dream, cause, ministry (or whatever you want to call it)? I hope to encourage you as I share my journey through that discovery process...

IT IS IN YOUR HEART

He has made everything beautiful and appropriate in its time. ***He has also planted eternity [a sense of divine purpose] in the human heart*** *[a mysterious longing which nothing under the sun can satisfy, except God]—yet man cannot find out [comprehend, grasp] what God has done [His overall plan] from the beginning to the end. (Ecclesiastes 3:11, Amplified Bible)*

"Then I arose in the night, I and a few men with me; I told no one what my God ***had put in my heart to do*** *at Jerusalem; nor was there any animal with me, except the one on which I rode." (Nehemiah 2:12)*

God has put your divine purpose in your heart. The first step is to search your heart.

I believe that just as the Lord knew your purpose before you were born, He also placed that purpose in your heart.

As I mentioned in Chapter Two, young children may already know what they like to do and what they would like to be when they get older. They might not be able to put it into words, given that their experience or vocabulary may be limited, but it is all in there.

For some people it might be easier to express because they have been exposed to certain elements of their dream and therefore can visualize or relate to it. They may have seen role models in their lives such as their parents, teachers, a military personnel, presidents, beauty queens or those in other professions.

Sometimes as people grow older, things may interfere with the dream in their heart; certain relationships or circumstances can act as either a stimulant or a hindrance to that dream.

The Bible says that Solomon successfully accomplished all that came into his heart to make in the house of the Lord and in his own house. (2 Chronicles 7:11) In his case, nothing interfered with that dream coming to pass.

So I searched my heart!

I sought to discover what I dreamt of becoming—what I saw myself doing in the future.

I took note of my dreams, no matter how possible or impossible they seemed; whether I was able to express them or not. I also took note of the things I loved doing.

As a young girl I noticed that I desired to see people well and happy. At that age I figured the only career I could pursue to fulfill that desire was a career as a doctor. But then my dream of becoming a doctor was crushed when I was told that in order to become a medical doctor I would need to perform surgery on a millipede—which I abhorred.

So much for that career!

Meanwhile I loved the Lord very much and wanted to be closer to Him. Growing up I watched how devoted my mom was to God, she was very dedicated to prayer and took her religion very seriously. Therefore, I learned to be the same way. With my limited experience, I concluded that the only way I could be very close to the Lord, was to become a nun. (That was my Catholic background kicking in.)

Then the nun plan came to naught when I became a Born Again Christian and joined a Pentecostal church.

As I searched, I realized I enjoyed encouraging people.

I still do! I love helping them and am willing to go the extra mile to bring a smile to their faces. As I looked back on my life experience, this trait sometimes got me in trouble as I began to please man rather than God. It took me a while to acknowledge and correct that tendency.

Along with the desire to encourage, I also realized that I had a strong desire to write; this had been in me from my childhood, and no matter how I tried, I could not shake it off.

I wrote my first story at the age of seven. It was about a young girl who was struck by a vehicle, and that girl was me. I still remember that piece to this day—probably because of the circumstances surrounding it. Some people stumbled upon my story and I was teased because it had quite a few spelling errors.

My story became a laughingstock.

The next time I would pick up a pen to write again was twenty years later.

Such is the discouraging effect that teasing or negativity can have on a person's life dream. But that second time, I had a more positive experience.

As I reflected on my life, I was reminded of the joy I felt when writing letters of encouragement to friends and acquaintances. Also whenever I needed to share my opinion about an important issue to individuals, I found it easier to communicate or express myself through writing. Those were things that stood out to me during my search.

Have you searched your heart? If you haven't, it's not too late to start.

Also you don't have to travel far to find what's inside.

Take time to reflect back through your life and discover your likes and dislikes, your early thoughts about what you might have wanted to do or be.

You may not have placed much value on your

passions until now, but they do often reveal what you're called to do in your life.

After you have discovered what is in your heart, do not despise it no matter how little it may seem; just trust the Lord with it. If the Lord can trust you with a little, then He can trust you with much. (Zechariah 4:10; Luke 19:17)

GOD'S DIRECTION REVEALED

Trust God with ALL your heart; lean not on your own understanding, and He will direct your paths. (Proverbs 3:5 & 6)

Years ago the Lord allowed me to see this verse in a different way. He revealed to me that as I trusted Him with all my heart and with everything, also as I acknowledged Him in all my ways and in everything I did, then I would realize that my paths were already being directed by Him.

As you trust the Lord and acknowledge Him in everything, you too may realize that your path has already been leading you into your calling. It is not so much that your paths will begin to be directed, but that you will come to a realization that your path has *already been* directed because you acknowledged Him.

To acknowledge God is to accept His existence; it is also to recognize and confess His importance in your life.

If, even after a heart search, you are not aware of what is in your heart, ask the Lord to reveal it to you and He will.

He may show you in several ways. At times you might need someone else to help you understand what is in your heart. When Samuel anointed Saul as king of Israel, he also told him *all that was in his heart*. In other words, Samuel prophesied over Saul. He told Saul ahead of time that he would be king, and also shared specific things he would encounter as a confirmation. (I Samuel 9:19)

Prophecies can be helpful road signs along our path...

PROPHECIES AND CONFIRMATIONS

*Do not quench the Spirit. **Do not despise prophecies**. Test all things; hold fast what is good. Abstain from every form of evil. (1 Thessalonians 5:19-21)*

Believe in the Lord your God, and you shall be established; believe His prophets, and you shall prosper." *(2 Chronicles 20:20)*

I love to view the above scripture this way: Do you want 20/20 vision, spiritually? Well the Bible gives it to us in 2 Chronicles **20:20**.

The Lord may send people into your life to confirm your calling or purpose.

Personally I have experienced that kind of prophetic encouragement. Several people (including friends) told me they believed I would be a pastor's wife. At the time, I disagreed with them because I had yet to accept it.

But they were right!

At times, prophecies can reveal something new to you; however they can also (and more often) confirm what is already in your heart. At the very least, something should "resonate" with your spirit when you receive a prophecy, even if you don't know how it will come about.

After the minister prophesies to you, you might begin to realize the reason you had certain dreams or desires. The prophecy can help you feel more confident going in a certain direction, and you may feel bold enough to take the next steps.

There are other things that can help you feel more

confident as well—God's revelation can come straight to you through dreams and visions, or it can come through other means such as counselors, classes and personality tests...

DREAMS, COUNSELORS, QUESTIONNAIRES, SEMINARS

*Where there is no counsel, the people fall; **but in the multitude of counselors there is safety.** (Proverbs 11:14)*

In addition to prophecies from servants of God, confirmation can also come through dreams, workshops, questionnaires and other helpful self-discovery tools.

God can reveal your purpose to you through dreams, while you're asleep. At times you might need someone to help you interpret them, but at other times you might be able to get a sense of what the dream is trying to reveal.

The Lord revealed Joseph's purpose through his dreams. Although Joseph got in trouble for sharing his dream to the wrong people, at the end of the day *God still worked it out* and his dream came to pass.

Isn't it amazing how God chooses times when we are asleep to work out things in our lives?

Do you recall Adam being *asleep* when God took out a rib to create Eve?

How about Abraham and the covenant that the Lord cut with him while he slept? (Genesis 15:12-21)

Our soul has a tendency to resist being still, so often God works in us while our minds are quieter. His methods of communication may not be what we expect.

Just as his revelation to Elijah came in a still small voice after he ran from Jezebel (1 Kings 19:12), so God works in all sorts of ways that may not show up with loud fireworks but might appear to us more quietly.

I recall times when the Lord gave me dreams that shed some light on my calling.

Once I dreamt that I was in a church. In the dream, everyone was asleep and I was about to go to sleep as well, but as soon as I did, we were attacked by a band of thieves who robbed us and destroyed a lot of things.

I was concerned when I had this dream. But after praying and sharing it with one of my mentors, we realized it came as a confirmation that one of my life's callings was prayer and intercession. I often share this story because it made such a difference in my life.

Before my marriage, I had another dream that made a huge difference in my life. It came during a critical time when I was in doubt about my calling as a pastor's wife.

My husband and I had just begun our relationship and we did believe it would end up in marriage. Then we had a major misunderstanding (to put it nicely).

What do you think was the cause?

He had shared with me what he believed was his calling- -to become a pastor. And if you hadn't noticed already, being a pastor's wife was definitely not in my plans. Therefore, since I knew I loved him, naturally I tried to talk him out of it. (You can imagine how nicely that conversation went!)

Let's just say it didn't end very well. I left convinced this was the end of our relationship.

But that night I had a dream. In the dream I saw my husband-to-be as a pastor of a church, ministering in such a powerful way. When I woke up I knew for sure that he was right.

Then the question was—did I want to be part of this or not?

That was the question in my heart when I woke up that morning.

Do you know what else was in my heart that morning? The fact that I had to humble myself and say to him, "You were right."

The dream spoke directly to what I was going through and brought clarity into that situation. Through this dream I finally became convinced that I *was* called to be a pastor's wife.

I still had a choice to follow God's will or to go against it (and the battle was not over), but the dream did help nudge me in the right direction.

At times you might be privileged to attend conferences, workshops, programs or seminars that have been organized to help people discover their purpose. You might get to fill out some questionnaires or take tests that help you find out more about your personality, temperament and spiritual gifts. As it is with prophetic words, these can help confirm things you might already suspect and point you in the right direction.

As you now know, I struggled with my gifts for a while and could not understand why I was the way I was. I had a lot of questions about my personality and why I did things "differently." I viewed myself as being too soft.

I was determined to change until I went through a leadership-training program and was required to take one of those tests. It was then I discovered that I had the gift of *compassion!*

And all the while there I was trying to suppress something that God had given me!

Yes, I had tried to suppress my gift because of the trials and painful experiences I'd gone through; I understood why. But that test helped me see a bigger picture and purpose at work in my life.

Discovering the bigger picture not only helped me stop trying to change who I was, but also helped me accept my gift, be thankful for it and walk in it.

LIFE'S TRIALS & EXPERIENCES

*My brethren, count it all joy when **you fall into various trials, knowing that the testing of your faith produces patience**. But let patience have its perfect work, that you may be perfect and complete, lacking nothing.* (James 1:2-4)

[But the Lord rebukes Jeremiah's impatience, saying] If you have raced with men on foot and they have tired you out, then how can you compete with horses? And if [you take to flight] in a land of peace where you feel secure, then what will you do [when you tread the tangled maze of jungle haunted by lions] in the swelling and flooding of the Jordan? (Jeremiah 12:5, Amp.)

Certain trials or situations we go through can often indicate our purpose or calling. I encourage you to examine those trials and you will notice some lessons that may be linked to your purpose.

God allows these struggles not to torture us, but to strengthen us. Through them we learn lessons and acquire certain attributes that we need to fulfill our purpose.

Even if the trials come due to the enemy's attempt to thwart our purpose, or due to our own lusts (James 1:13 &14), God still turns things around so that they work to prepare us for our purpose.

I now accept that God graced me with the gift of compassion. However before I understood this, I fought against it because I was tired of being hurt.

You see, I loved it when people were happy, and so I

thought it was my duty to make or keep them happy. (Have you ever tried to keep everyone happy? It's exhausting!)

If being quiet made them happy, I became quiet. If being jovial kept them happy then I tried to be jovial. In my attempt to please people and be accepted, I lost myself and became depressed because I felt rejected.

I had twisted my own gift to fit a people-pleasing mode. Just as Moses had first tried to work out his gift in his own way, I'd done the same. Then, due to all the rejection, I ran away from using my gifts. I made conscious efforts *not* to be compassionate. (That didn't work out so well either.)

What I needed to do was to put things in the right perspective: I needed to first love and please God and then love people.

"The first and greatest commandment is to love God with all your heart, soul and mind and strength; the second is to love your neighbor as yourself." (Matthew 22:37-39)

Perhaps these commandments are presented in that order for a reason!

It's amazing how much difference perspective makes. As a young child you are exposed to certain situations that influence you to view the world a certain way. The things you are exposed to during those years often determine how you will relate (or not relate) to certain circumstances.

For instance, many years ago, I watched as a visitor to the U.S. was offered soda to drink. He responded, "No thanks."

I'm an inquisitive person, so I asked him why.

As it turns out, he was unfamiliar with our language and had no clue what "soda" was.

I mention this because it's important for us to be aware that our experience may be different from another's. The influences in our lives shape our view.

Just as I first thought the only way for me to express

my devotion to God was to become a nun, so you may have certain ideas of how your calling will play out.

But be prepared to be surprised, as I was on my journey. When I went away to boarding school and became a Born-Again Christian, my view of life's options changed significantly.

Your upbringing, exposures, experiences...definitely all come together at some point to play a major role in your life's purpose...and when you love God, all things work together for good. (Romans 8:28) For instance, I remember my mom always prayed with us when we were growing up. I didn't realize then why she did it or insisted on doing it, but I do now. Now, as I pray with my kids I realize how that experience shaped me.

The jobs you have held, both past and present, can also give you a sense of what your gifts or callings are. Particularly those jobs you loved.

Find out why you loved certain jobs. What was it about them that appealed to you?

When I think about the different jobs I have held—working as a cashier, in a hospital, in a bank, and finally working in the field of education—I can see different attributes I have gained from my experiences at these places that are so diverse.

Now I can see how they all worked together for good. I may not have known at the time how these things would all somehow contribute to my calling, but when I look back, they all contributed to my life training. In the same way, the people and ministries I have been drawn to in my life were also part of God's unique training for me.

MENTORS, MENTEES & MINISTRIES

Paul, an apostle of Jesus Christ, by the commandment of God our Savior and the Lord Jesus Christ, our hope, **to Timothy, a true son in the faith**: *Grace, mercy, and peace from God our Father and Jesus Christ our Lord. (1Timothy 1:1-2)*

Now it happened as they journeyed on the road, that someone said to Him, "Lord, **I will follow You wherever You go**.*" (Luke 9:57)*

Are you drawn to certain people or ministries? Are there those who you admire, those who you'd like to be around so that you could become more like them?

And on the other end, are you drawn to give to certain people? It's good to have a few at both ends—those who mentor you and those you can mentor.

The Lord brings people into your life, sometimes for a season, to guide you through certain situations. He also puts people in your life for you to help as they go through their situations and trials. Often the ones He gives you to help may have similar gifts, interests, convictions or causes as you do. This is no accident.

You will notice that David was brought into the palace to help the king, and later became king. Also the king's son Jonathan became a friend that David could admire; when King Saul wasn't a great role model, Jonathan was a great encouragement to David.

Have you ever been in a situation where you felt hurt by someone who was supposedly your mentor?

David went through this; he was under a hurtful mentor and God delivered him. If you find yourself in that situation, prayerfully consider your next step, *behave yourself wisely* and let the Lord lead you.

Sometimes it might be that we have put that mentor or

leader on a pedestal and placed unrealistic expectations on them. In that case we are devastated or hurt when they behave like any human being and either fail or hurt us. Eventually we need to learn to receive what's good and move on, or eat the meat and spit out the bones, as they say.

I am not suggesting that you disrespect or act meanly towards those mentors who have hurt you. Nor would I suggest that you be ungrateful to them; don't burn your bridges if you can help it. Pray for wisdom as to how you might handle your situation. Be humble and the Lord will direct you just as He did with David.

Most importantly, be forgiving and allow the Lord to heal you of the hurt from that relationship so you are not hindered in your walk with Him.

But be encouraged. You will also find many healthy examples of mentoring in the Scriptures.

ELIJAH & ELISHA

Elisha was not only a servant to Elijah; he was also mentored by him. Later when Elijah was taken up into the clouds, Elisha ended up with a double portion of his anointing.

PAUL & TIMOTHY

Another mentoring example is the relationship between Paul and Timothy. Paul referred to Timothy as his "son in the faith."

JETHRO & MOSES

There is also that of Moses and his father-in-law. Jethro gave Moses very important advice as he judged the Israelites during their journey through the wilderness. Moses heeded this advice because it came from an authentic and respected source.

There were others in the land of Midian, but God led Moses after he fled from Egypt to Reuel, the Priest of Midian.

Moses ended up being not only a deliverer and judge but a priest as well. (Exodus 18:19-26)

Mentors offer guidance and counsel so that you do not have to make the same mistakes they did, or fall into traps you may not have noticed.

Just as your various jobs can help give you an idea of your calling or purpose, the ministries you are part of can do the same. I noticed that there were certain ministries I was drawn to—those I especially loved. There were even certain programs I wanted to watch, those that had to do with certain kinds of ministry. All these things helped give me a sense of my calling.

Maybe that's you too. Perhaps you watched a certain ministry broadcast, and you were able to identify with that particular ministry without being able to explain why. It could be that you feel a deep sense to serve in or help with that ministry.

Whatever the case may be, take note of those situations; they can point you in the right direction.

When David was sent by his father to take his brothers some food, he got to the place of battle and he heard Goliath's rant. Something *clicked* in him that stirred him to join the battle and destroy this giant that had the nerve to defile the army of the living God.

Although his brother accused him of having an ulterior motive, his response to that was, "Is there not a cause?" (I Samuel 17:29) He was moved by this cause because he wanted to glorify God. He could not stand to see the armies of God defiled, and he was moved not only by selfish ambition.

As you observe a ministry, if something within you connects with that ministry, then it is worth praying about it.

Seek God's face in that matter. As you watch others minister, if you can identify with them, or if something clicks inside of you (you see yourself preaching, singing, serving, ushering...) again check your motive. Seek the Lord concerning it and take note of it.

The main thing to remember is that if it is from God, it will lead you in a direction that glorifies God.

Even if you don't always know for sure how to discern what's right to do, your godly choices will prove themselves by their fruit.

Have you noticed how your attention works after you've purchased a new car, how suddenly you begin to see cars like yours everywhere you go? It might seem strange; those same cars probably crossed your path so many other times before but you never noticed them until you bought an identical car...

I believe something similar is at work when it comes to our callings. What God has put inside of you bears witness to the others around you who are ministering in the same areas.

In other words: **Your spirit within you leaps up in recognition when you encounter something you are called to be or do, just like John the Baptist leapt in Elizabeth's womb when greeted by Mary the mother of Jesus.**

At times, you may also notice that you are drawn to ministries that others might have no interest in pursuing. Do not let this discourage you. It is a result of various gifting.

Ruth decided to go with Naomi although Orpah her sister-in-law did not. God had put such a determination in her that she said, *"Entreat me not to leave you, or to turn back from following after you; for wherever you go, I will go; and wherever you lodge, I will lodge; your people shall be my people, and your God, my God. Where you did, I will die, and there will I be buried. The LORD do so to me, and more also, if anything but death parts you and me." (Ruth 1:14-18)*

Strong words! They come from the heart of Ruth's calling to follow the God of her mother-in-law Naomi.

Does it surprise you that some could be interested in certain careers or things you would consider insane?

The first time I read the job description of an air traffic controller, I was convinced no one in his or her right mind would desire such a job! To my surprise, however, there are. (And good thing, too, for the rest of us who ride on the planes.)

Once I heard of a doctor who wanted to be assigned to the worst cases in a trauma unit and would not have it any other way; what a contrast to those who literally pass out at the sight of gore.

It is God's plan that we aren't all made the same way—you can rejoice in that!

There were a few ladies I was particularly close to when growing up in the Lord in a certain season of my life. I later realized, as I looked back over the years, that they were mostly wives of pastors. If not at that time, then later in life they became pastor's wives.

My friends and I often find it amusing whenever we reflect on my refusal to accept my calling as a pastor's wife; they knew all along what the end would be. The Lord knew what He was doing all that time; it was not until I hit rock bottom that I stopped running and decided to accept His will for my life.

Those desires and dreams were in me all along. My suppressing them didn't stop God from reaching me eventually. True, I'd decided I could marry an evangelist, a teacher, or any minister in the church (*anyone*) but a pastor) and then I would be safe and not have to go through too much pain and rejection.

That was my conclusion, but it didn't really hold water.

My calling was not based on what I wanted to do but what I needed to do.

A NEED OR CAUSE VS. A WANT

And David said, "What have I done now? Is there not a cause?" (1 Samuel 17:29)

"The Spirit of the LORD is upon Me, because He has anointed Me to preach the gospel to the poor; He has sent Me to heal the brokenhearted, to proclaim liberty to the captives and recovery of sight to the blind, to set at liberty those who are oppressed; to proclaim the acceptable year of the LORD." (Luke 4:18-19)

"Therefore I remind you to stir up the gift of God which is in you through the laying on of my hands." (2 Timothy 1:6)

In the previous section I mentioned that my calling was not based on what I wanted to do but what I needed to do.

How is that?

A need helps to point you in the right direction:

- There is a need that you see, a gap of sorts—a vacuum that draws your attention. It's something that others may overlook, while it feels to you more like *a cause*.
- And then there is a need you feel within; it is more like a pull to *do* something, regardless of your past experience; this is an inner *drive*.

Although these two aspects of a "need" might seem different, they are two sides of the same coin and can reveal what direction you are to take.

Your purpose may come in form of a need you see in the world; it's a cause that calls out to you.

David recognized a cause when he witnessed the need to deliver God's people from their enemies. As he heard Goliath defy the armies of the living God, he was stirred up to do something about it.

Even when rebuked by his older brother, David responded, *"Is there not a cause?"* We know how the story ends; he went on to kill the giant and led Israel to victory, long before he became king.

David saw a need; he also felt the need to do something about it, and it propelled him in the direction of his purpose.

So it is with your purpose. You may feel it in form of a drive, a need, or an urge to act. You may be drawn to it yet also inclined to keep your distance, maybe as a result of past events. For example, as it was with me you might be moved to help people but also reluctant because of the hurt you've experienced.

How about Joseph or Ruth? They each could have chosen to keep their distance from the things that reminded them of pain and hurt. Instead, they pressed on because they were motivated by a need—a spiritual drive—not their wants.

Ruth went through the grief of losing her husband, brother-in-law and father-in-law. Some would want to separate themselves from all that loss, yet she was compelled to go with Naomi wherever she went. She ended up marrying Boaz and becoming part of the genealogy of Christ.

Joseph had dreams that he interpreted and shared. Though it was a gift, it initially led to him being sold into slavery and imprisoned. He had a pretty good reason to stay away from interpreting dreams at that point. And besides, his dream about his brothers hadn't come to pass yet.

However he didn't give it up but chose to interpret dreams

even in prison. How did that help? Later on the butler (a former prison inmate whose dream he had interpreted) recommended him to Pharaoh. Which, in turn, led to Joseph becoming second in command in Egypt.

Then Jesus was led up by the Spirit into the wilderness to be tempted by the devil. And when He had fasted forty days and forty nights, afterward He was hungry. (Matthew 4:1 & 2)

As Jesus began His ministry at the age of thirty, the Spirit led Him every step of the way to help Him fulfill His purpose—even leading Him into the wilderness where His authority was challenged and proved.

The Holy Spirit will lead you as well, helping you recognize the need, and also driving you to do something about it. Holy Spirit will help stir up the cause inside of you and compel you to action.

A want is what's *desired*; a need is what's *required*.

You might want a specific thing but not necessarily need it.

Remember my desire to sing? After much heart examination, I had to be honest with myself: singing for me was what I wanted—something I wished I could do because I loved music—not what I felt I *needed* to do in order to be fulfilled.

If you are going through a similar situation, examine your heart and check your motives. **Invite the Lord to search your heart, to reveal the motive behind those wants.**

Take the instance of a young man who watches a minister on T.V and wants to preach like that minister. How does he differentiate between a need and a want in this case?

My answer would be for him to **check his motive**. Why does he have the desire to preach like him?

Is it so he can be seen by men, or is it to bring glory to God by touching lives? It might be a mixture of both.

The main thing is that you be honest with yourself.

Sometimes you can tell the difference by simply answering this question: Is it something I want or is it something I just see myself doing, regardless of what I want? Always check the origin, the motive, the *why*... of your desire.

And even when you cannot tell the difference, God sees your heart and works it out. If you find yourselves in a situation where you acted out of ignorance, He has a way of helping you. After all, He knows we are not perfect.

A lady I know, once found herself in a relationship that she honestly thought was God's plan for her. The relationship fell apart, and later as she looked back on it, she admitted some mistakes that she'd made, decisions based on her own selfish plans.

We had a lengthy discussion about this, and at the end I had to assure her that the Lord knew her heart. He knew that she did not set out in her heart to go against Him.

The truth is that He is omniscient; He knows everything! He knows when our desire is to first glorify Him, and when it is more of a *what's-in-it-for-me* plan.

He knows when we make an honest mistake, and even a foolish and harmful mistake out of lust, like David did.

He knows when we purposely go against His plan to pursue our self-justifying plan, like Jonah did.

And yes we do suffer consequences for our actions, but if we are repentant and stay in God, He works it out.

What's important is that we are after His heart and honest about what's in ours.

If and when you realize you are headed the wrong way, stop, turn around, get back in line and let Him lead you. God works in mysterious ways!

Let no one say when he is tempted, "I am tempted by God," for God cannot be tempted by evil, nor does He Himself tempt anyone. But each one is tempted when he is drawn away by his own desires and enticed. (James 1:13-14)

Needs and wants can both come in form of desires, but it's important to be able to discern the difference between them; it's the difference between your flesh and your spirit.

A friend of mine shared how she fought with her calling to be pastor and tried to negotiate with the Lord. She thought she could get away from it by marrying a pastor.

However there was still a struggle deep within, and she could not get away from that call. She finally surrendered, is now pastoring a church and has touched so many lives. In her case, initially she did not have a desire to be a pastor, but did feel a deep need to be a pastor. You might try to deny it, distort it, cover it up or compromise but no joy or fulfillment comes from that.

Your purpose is a need that pulls and draws you, and if left unanswered, it leaves you with a void.

In some cases people chase after positions and titles; however I learned that it's not necessary to chase after those things.

As you seek and chase after the *LORD*, those things will chase after you.

Years ago when I attended grad school, I had the opportunity to be part of a Bible study group. The couple who coordinated the group was about to move to another state. Desiring that the group continue, they asked if I could help lead it.

I was not ready for such responsibility, therefore my response was, "I will pray about it." Everything told me to run and never return, but deep down there was a little voice that reminded me of the pull I had inside of me.

One thing I have realized is that whenever we are

presented with a need and God is nudging us to fulfill it, He has also equipped us for it. Hence the pull from within. (He had already equipped me, whether I knew it or not.)

Finally I was done "praying about it"... and stepped up. The Lord has blessed that Bible study and kept it going all this time.

IT WILL REQUIRE YOUR GIFT

Then the LORD spoke to Moses, saying, "See, I have called by name Bezalel the son of Uri, the son of Hur, of the tribe of Judah. And I have filled him with the Spirit of God, in wisdom, in understanding, in knowledge, and in all manner of workmanship, to design artistic works, to work in gold, in silver, in bronze, in cutting jewels for setting, in carving wood, and to work in all manner of workmanship. (Exodus 30:1-5)

Every good gift and every perfect gift is from above, and comes down from the Father of lights, with whom there is no variation or shadow of turning. (James 1:17)

I believe the best way to get direction with regard to your purpose is to find out what your gifts are. Your purpose will always require your gift.

You may think that your gift and their purpose are one and the same, but that is not the case. Your gift is part of your purpose; it's the tool God uses in you to help carry out your purpose.

Proverbs 18:16 says that **a man's gift makes room for him and brings him before great men**.

You may find that your gifts are easier to identify than your purpose. The gifts may give you an indication of what area in life you need to focus on.

For instance, if you draw very well, your gift is to draw but your purpose is where drawing takes you. You could end up as an architect, artist, art teacher, designer or an art therapist.

I am convinced that in most cases, people have knowledge of their gifts but lack the knowledge of their purpose. In other cases, they might be aware of both but choose to use their gifts outside of their purpose to receive worldly gain.

We see this in the story of Samson; he was aware of his gift and his purpose but chose to use his gift for a selfish purpose. (Judges 16) He was still impressive, but his story doesn't end well.

A lady might be blessed with a beautiful voice; that is a gift. She then needs to find out how to use her voice to glorify God; that is purpose. Use your gifts to bring people into the kingdom of God to His glory. That's an awesome purpose.

If you are not aware of your purpose, use your gifts prayerfully and humbly, acknowledge God while you do, and you will be led to your purpose.

If you are not sure of your gifts, begin by identifying those things that bring you contentment, things you absolutely love to do; something you could do with joy, without caring if you got paid for it or not.

Another helpful indicator is to take note of those things that cause you to be broken.

For me it was the compassion.

Just being a compassionate person, I get stepped on very often— but I choose to stay compassionate even though it brings me pain and brokenness.

Using your gift requires brokenness, but that's not a bad thing. Brokenness keeps you humble before God and that is crucial.

Remember, your gift will bring you before great men. *Your purpose will keep you there!*

I used to compare myself to others a lot and it took me a

while to realize that I needed to quit doing that. There was a time in my life when the Lord was leading me to not do certain things, and I would complain to Him: "But so-and-so does that and she (or he) is a very strong Christian so why can't I?"

Oh, the questions we ask sometimes! Thank God for His mercies!

I had to learn to keep my focus on the Lord and what I was called to do, not be discouraged by the fact that I couldn't do what everyone else was doing. My focus wasn't supposed to be on "everyone else" but on the Lord.

FOCUS SOLELY ON THE LORD

Therefore we also, since we are surrounded by so great a cloud of witnesses, let us lay aside every weight, and the sin which so easily ensnares us, and let us run with endurance the race that is set before us, ***looking unto Jesus, the Author and Finisher of our faith,*** *Who for the joy that was set before Him endured the cross, despising the shame, and has sat down at the right hand of the throne of God.* (Hebrews 12:1-2)

So He said, "Come." And when Peter had come down out of the boat, he walked on water to go to Jesus. But ***when he saw that the wind was boisterous, he was afraid;*** *and beginning to sink he cried out, saying, "Lord, save me!"* (Matthew 14:29-30)

If you remember nothing else from this book, the simplest thing you can remember is to keep your focus on God at all times.

When you look at the passage from Matthew, you'll see Jesus' invitation to Peter: "Come." Even though there were many on the boat, Peter was the only one who asked the Lord to prove himself, so he received the invitation.

"Many are called but few are chosen." (Matthew 22:14)

Remember this verse from the previous chapter? Peter's boldness as he asked questions and stepped out of the boat illustrates it well. The chosen few are not some mysterious elite; they are simply **those who choose to respond to His call.**

They are the ones who are willing to step out of their comfort zones and weather life's storms with Jesus.

Peter stepped out by faith, but then as soon as he took his eyes off Jesus and focused on the "boisterous" wind, he began to sink. That boisterous wind might be various trials in your life, challenging relationships or other experiences. It might be your shortcomings or those of others.

Personally, I've noticed that the minute I take my eyes off Jesus, I get discouraged instantly.

On the other hand, even in stormy seasons, as long as I keep my eyes on Him I have felt great peace.

Your focus on the Lord is crucial for several reasons. Not only does it help prevent you from sinking in over your head in turbulent times, but it's also about the uniqueness of your calling.

We are all different; sometimes you will find that others can do things you can't do while you can do things others can't do. That's the way He created us.

The Lord may use many different ways to help you discover your purpose. Whether you're in the midst of a storm or simply pursuing your own calling, keep focused on Jesus no matter what, and you will rise above distractions to fulfill what you're born to do.

CHAPTER 8

Birthing Your Purpose

Who has heard such a thing? Who has seen such things? Shall the earth be made to give birth in one day? Or shall a nation be born at once? For as soon as Zion was in labor, she gave birth to her children. (Isaiah 66:8)

If you faint in the day of adversity, your strength is small. (Proverbs 24:10)

The word "birthing" means *the act or process of bringing forth or bearing offspring.*

In order to give birth, one has to be pregnant, and pregnancy cannot take place without a seed. Your purpose is that seed placed in you from the moment you came into being. (Psalm 139:16)

In addition, a biological mother does not choose who her child is going to be; neither does the child choose her parents. Likewise, you do not get to choose your purpose or your dream. You can recognize it and honor it and embrace it, but you didn't put it in there; God did.

In order for you to birth your purpose, it does help to identify what it what it is. After reading Chapter 7, you may be closer to identifying your purpose than you were before.

Then you have the privilege of entering the preparation

process in earnest. In Chapter 5, I made a brief mention of the changes involved in pregnancy as it relates to your preparation. In this chapter we will look more closely at what's involved in birthing your purpose.

CHANGES

When I ponder the word "birthing," I cannot help but think about the huge changes an expectant mother goes through. We know she goes through a lot of *physical* changes before bringing forth her child. (WebMD, Baby Center, Health line) In turn, you can derive many *spiritual* implications from these changes when applied to birthing your purpose.

For the guys reading this, there is no need to be nervous. I once heard a preacher say that when he got married he was a groom, however when Jesus (the Bridegroom) comes, he would be a bride.

If women can be "sons" in the Lord, then men can be the "bride of Christ." God transcends gender! However for those of you who plan to be married and have kids, you will be grateful for this chapter.

- One of the changes an expectant mother goes through is the ***respiratory system*** change. She experiences a *rise in respiratory rate* in order to compensate for the increased maternal oxygen. The respiratory system has to do with your breathing: As you get ready to birth your purpose, **you need more of the breath of God!** You get that increased breath by spending more time in His presence, with the Holy Spirit and really receiving from Him—in prayer, worship, fellowship, and the word. *And when*

He had said this, He breathed on them, and said to them, "Receive the Holy Spirit. (John 20:22)

- Then there is the **cardiovascular system** change. There is an increase in blood volume and *the heart* is enlarged for increased cardiac output; it also accommodates the pressure of the expanding womb on the veins. As you prepare to birth your purpose, you may begin to go through diverse trials and temptations. These situations put you through intense pressure that can cause brokenness; and ideally **this leads to greater humility and submission to God**. In other words, your heart of hearts really gets a workout. The more God uses you, the greater humility you need. *But in all things we commend ourselves as ministers of God: in much patience, in tribulations, in needs, in distresses, in stripes, in imprisonments, in tumults, in labors, in sleeplessness, in fastings. (2 Corinthians 6:4 & 5)*

- We also have the **gastrointestinal system** change. This involves the *displacement* of an expectant mother's stomach, intestine and other organs as the womb enlarges. Everything gets rearranged! Similarly, when your purpose begins to expand, certain things get displaced in your life. You might begin to go through shifts—less time is spent on unimportant and unprofitable things, certain friends or circles begin to break off—**priorities get rearranged in your life,** not necessarily by a conscious effort on your part.

This rearranging is similar to the pruning process. When trees or vines are pruned, certain (dormant and dead) branches are cut off so that nourishment is focused on fewer branches in order to bear richer, more succulent fruit or prettier flowers. The best time to prune trees is right before new buds come in—in other words, right before they bear fruit. In the same way, **you may get pruned right before you birth your purpose.**

The gastrointestinal system also involves the process of *elimination*. You take in a lot, and your digestive system works to eliminate waste. In relation to birthing your purpose, you may notice that life is filled with lots of experiences-good and bad, useful and useless, fruitful and unfruitful. **The Holy Spirit works with your spirit to help you discern the difference and eliminate what is not needful.** *Every branch in Me that does not bear fruit He takes away; and every branch that bears fruit He prunes, that it may bear more fruit. (John. 15:2)*

- The ***musculoskeletal system*** change involves a *realignment* of the spinal curvature; this occurs in order to provide support and maintain balance in the expectant mother. It is appropriate that after certain things have been eliminated and other things added, there is a need for realignment in your life. **I believe that in order to maintain balance, the Lord brings people into our lives to help support and train us, and He brings other people into our lives so we can help them**. *"Freely you have received, freely give."*

The body of Christ works like an actual body, with Christ as the head and we in alignment as the rest of His body. The body needs the head and the head needs the body. (Remember that you are needed!) As we work together, bearing with one another in love, the strong bearing the weak, we promote unity in the body. And we get better realigned with Him as we line up with one another in Him. In Him we live, move and have our being.

Are you aware that people are strategically placed in your path to help you grow and bring your purpose to birth? Talk about divine connections! Another thing: when God places someone in your life to help you birth that purpose, He knows exactly who you need. You might not like everything they do, but you need to love them and honor them as you would a parent. Those who mentor you are like spiritual parents to you; they may also be spiritual midwives in your life to help you birth your spiritual baby—that purpose, that ministry, that dream. *We then who are strong ought to bear with the scruples of the weak, and not to please ourselves. (Romans 15:1)*

- An expectant mom also goes through **abdominal** changes. This *enlargement* of the abdomen is the most obvious and visible change, caused by the growth of the fetus. Quite literally, the baby begins to take up more space. The spiritual relevance is that as you get ready to birth your purpose, your vision gets larger, it develops, and its territory begins to expand. **It takes up more of your time and space**. That purpose begins to consume you; you eat, drink, go to sleep and wake up with it. Also at that point people around you may notice a difference in you—that you're full of God and on the brink of something new. *And his disciples remembered that it was written, The zeal of thine house hath eaten me up (John 2:17)*
- Finally, another phenomenon an expectant mother goes through is **skin** changes. Her skin begins to develop stretch marks, or *scars caused by stretching.* She may experience increased discomfort, cramps or

pain caused by the growth of the baby. As you prepare to birth your purpose, **you will be stretched; you will face opposition, you will go through pain, and you will go through hurts and betrayals, which will leave scars**. But do not be discouraged! God's grace is sufficient for you. And they can become glorified scars. The good thing about glorified scars is they are like what Jesus had, and they help people like Thomas believe that you've "been there." *And lest I should be exalted above measure by the abundance of the revelations, a thorn in the flesh was given to me, a messenger of Satan to buffet me, lest I be exalted above measure (2 Corinthians 12: 7)*

Prepared or Premature?

Just as the mother goes through changes, the baby also goes through changes. The process a baby goes through prepares it to survive outside the womb.

Similarly, from the time God's seed is planted in your heart to the time of birthing your purpose, it too goes through a process geared to help your purpose survive in the world.

However, many people are not patient enough to go through the process.

Take for instance babies who are born prematurely. If they do survive, it may not be without some kind of intervention. We cannot ignore the amount of care and effort that doctors and nurses put in to ensure that the child not only survives but also lives a normal life.

The risks are similar if your dream or purpose is birthed prematurely. Therefore it is imperative that you go through the process.

After being birthed prematurely, some dreams have had to lie in an incubator for a while.

Far worse, some have been aborted (intentionally or unintentionally) and have not survived.

Acting before your time and not wanting to go through the PROCESS is premature birthing and can cost you your dream unless the Lord intervenes.

In the Bible you can find instances of God's intervention in the lives of His people such as Moses (Exodus 2:11-14) and Jacob (Genesis 25:31, Genesis 27:19) Never despise the process you have to go through—it adds to your dream.

Just like a baby who spends the last few weeks in the womb, building fat deposits which will be needed after leaving the womb to keep warm, our process prepares us.

When going through little trials that prepare you for bigger ones, do not give up. Your purpose will be brought to "full term" and be stronger for it.

MISCARRIAGE AND ABORTIONS

Many dreams and purposes have been miscarried because time was not taken to go through God's processes.

Some have even aborted their purpose and dreams because they did not know the value of what they were carrying. Carry your purpose with care and value it so you do not lose it.

There was a point in my life when the Lord began dealing with me about *process.* He wanted to reveal its importance to me. I was led to the book of Ezekiel, where the prophet was told to prophesy to the dry bones in the valley. The Bible says Ezekiel prophesied to them to live. After he spoke to the bones, they began to come together. Then sinews came on the bones... then flesh... then the skin... and lastly, the breath. In other words, those dry bones had to go through a *process* or several stages before they became a mighty army. (Ezekiel 37: 7-10)

In life as we face trials and overcome them, we learn lessons, and then learn more lessons. As this happens, we are building ourselves up, one step at a time. A *process* helps you build upward (not downward). Therefore I urge you to view each life lesson as a building block.

The munitions you gather in the valley are essential while climbing the mountain.

Do not forget the lessons learned over the years or else you will need to learn them again! (Isaiah 28:9-13; Ezekiel 47:3-6; Mark 4:26-28; 2 Peter 1:5-7; Jude 1:20)

In my experience, there have been situations in which I got frustrated because things were not moving quickly enough. Have you ever felt like that? I tried to make things happen on my own and felt the need to open some doors myself—but it only led to frustration, hurt and broken hearts.

IT IS TIME

Earlier we discussed the concept of *time* playing a major role in fulfilling our purpose. The question is, how do you know when it is *time*?

When we were expecting our second child, my husband shared with me his desire to hear the words, "It is time" when I went into labor. He requested that I use those exact words when the moment came. However I must confess that when it *was* time, I disappointed him because the pains came with such intensity that his request was the last thing on my mind!

An expectant mother is not able to pick what time she goes into labor, unless of course it is an extenuating circumstance. It would be too convenient if that were the case. In fact, if you had a conversation with her, you would find out very quickly that one of her concerns would be when and where she would go into labor.

A relative of mine once needed to relocate in order to begin a new job. The only problem was, she was almost due—about nine months pregnant. Her desire was to have her baby before the move, so she did all she could physically to try to make that happen. She took walks, ate certain foods, asked for all kinds of advice so as to speed up the process of labor—all to no avail.

Unfortunately, one day during that time she was in an accident and was taken to the hospital. On hearing this, I was certain this was IT—there was no doubt in my mind that it was TIME and that her baby was going to be born.

However, the baby was still not delivered that day! About a week later her baby arrived. All I could conclude from this situation was that God dictates when it is time and not man. Sometimes we might say, "That baby came late," or "The baby came early," but that's just the comparison between our own human expectations or due date—and God's reality. I believe the baby comes when it's *time*!

We can do all kinds of things to try and make our time come quickly, but it is the Lord who has the final say.

With Lazarus, who had died and was buried before Jesus arrived, it seemed as though the Lord was four days late. But He was still on time. That is, God had resurrection plans that far surpassed people's ideas about Lazarus being healed. Just as babies arrive in God's time, Jesus also arrives at just the right time.

How can you tell when it is *time*? A mother knows it is time when the labor pains or contractions begin—when they are more frequent and consistent; also when her water breaks.

I read an article once that said, "No one knows what causes labor to start or when it will start, but several hormonal and physical changes may indicate the beginning of labor." In a spiritual sense we have similar experiences: Certain changes in the Spirit give you an indication that it is *time*. Some of those indicators are pain (brokenness) and open doors (breakthroughs).

BROKENNESS AND BREAKTHROUGHS

Your time! (Ecclesiastes. 3:1) There are certain things that begin to happen in the Spirit to indicate it's time to birth your purpose.

Pain and Brokenness

The pain I am talking about comes unexpectedly. It is not foreseen, and it is not caused by any predicted event other than the fact that it is time. In other words, there is no rhyme or reason, but an indication that you are about to birth your purpose.

This pain stands out; it is not like any other, and it is something beyond your control. You may be hit with trials on every side, and just when you think you are about to catch a break, you are hit again. If you hold on, press in and push through, you will birth that purpose. But if you give up, then that purpose will not be birthed at that time.

Have you noticed? We humans do not care for pain. We tend to do anything but go through the pain—we avoid it, run away from it, medicate it, gloss over it, you name it. However at times pain is needful, because it results in brokenness, and brokenness keeps us humble and fruitful.

Verily, verily, I say unto you, except a corn of wheat fall into the ground and die, it abideth alone: but if it die, it bringeth forth much fruit. (John 12:24 KJV)

I read about a little girl who had a medical condition: She could not feel pain. I thought to myself, how wonderful it must be for her. But then as I read further, I realized that even though pain is something none of us desires, it is actually needful.

You see, pain is a messenger. With this girl, there was no way of telling whenever something was wrong. If she had touched something hot or cut herself, she wouldn't know that she was burned or wounded. If she'd been able to feel the pain of a headache or a stomachache, then she could have communicated that. But without pain, it was more of a guessing game. They would discover a condition after it was much worse or even too late.

How do you feel about pain now? Next time you feel pain—spiritually or physically—maybe you can be thankful, because it reveals what needs to be fixed.

Some people have miscarried or aborted dreams and purposes because they feared pain. God will not fight or strive with us; He has a perfect will and plan. Meanwhile we have our own plans and we would rather execute our plans and desires so as to escape having to deal with the pain of brokenness.

Now My soul is troubled, and what shall I say? 'Father, save Me from this hour'? But for this purpose I came to this hour. ²⁸ Father, glorify Your name." John 12:27

Often God tries to warn us or stop us like He stopped Balaam, but when we refuse to listen, then He allows us to carry out our plan. Then why are we surprised or blame God when we reap the negative results? When it is time to birth a purpose, there is always pain! You will feel PAIN!

Jacob had to be broken as he wrestled with the Man.

A horse has to be broken before it can be used.

It was very interesting to learn about how a horse is

broken. According to one article, horses that are broken to follow their leader out of genuine *respect* are much more enjoyable than those that follow out of *fear*. (Wikipedia "How To Do Anything")

One of the most amazing stories I heard about this came from a minister. He shared the process he took a horse through when he was trying to save the horse from getting put down for being too wild.

Although the process seemed painful and involved brokenness, he knew it was necessary to save the life of the horse. I believe that just as a horse's loyalty to its leader depends on how broken it is, so does our loyalty to the Lord depends on how broken we are.

My conclusion is this: The amount of breaking a horse needs depends on how wild it is; and the amount of breaking we go through depends on how rebellious or yielding we are. God loves us and wants to use us. He also wants us to love and serve Him, not out of fright but out of reverence, hence the breaking He takes us through.

Sufferings, trials, pain... break us because it produces character. (Romans 5:3-5; 2 Timothy 2:3)

In the Spirit there has to be a breaking before your divine baby is birthed, just as it is in the physical when the amniotic sac ruptures (when the water breaks).

Let's say the Lord begins to open doors in certain areas of your life; this is what is known as breakthrough. When this occurs, your job is to walk through in obedience regardless of fear. These might be doors you had tried in the past to open yourself, or a goal you tried to achieve rapidly, but failed. You may feel hesitant because of past obstacles, but if it's time, you are to walk through.

As you know I fought with the Lord about being a pastor's wife, though almost everyone I was close to saw it in me.

Whenever it was shared with me, I rebelled ...until I was broken!

Remember in the last chapter when I mentioned that "the battle was not over" regarding my acceptance in being a Pastor's wife? Well the good news is that I *did* get married. But the bad news is that for a while I still rebelled in my heart. I dressed up and went to meetings, services and interviews with my husband. However, God knows the deep things; He knew I had not fully submitted.

I still remember to this day where I was when I got to my breaking point. The pain I was going through combined with God's word coming at me from all directions. I could not miss it! It came through the ministers, through the Bible—everywhere.

I remember saying, "Ok Lord, I surrender! I will do it."

Very soon after that, we were sent on our first assignment. Brokenness preceded my breakthrough.

YOUR ROLE!

But Jesus said to him, "No one, having put his hand to the plow, and looking back, is fit for the kingdom of God." (Luke 9:62)

Looking unto Jesus, the author and finisher of our faith, who for the joy that was set before Him endured the cross, despising the shame, and has sat down at the right hand of the throne of God. (Hebrews 12:2)

What is your Role? After you realize "It is time," what part do you play? You press, retreat, act and yield: P. R. A. Y. (Not necessarily in that order.) We cannot say enough about Prayer.

When it is time, brokenness leads you to pray.

God's people were supposed to spend 400 years in a foreign land according to the scriptures but they spent 430 years. *Why?*

When you travail in the place of prayer, you will bring forth fruit. The bible says, the Lord said to Moses, that He had heard *the cry* of His people. In other words, they began to cry out to the Lord for deliverance, for help and He heard them.

In the first year of his reign I, Daniel, understood by the books the number of the years specified by the word of the LORD through Jeremiah the prophet, that He would accomplish seventy years in the desolations of Jerusalem. Then I set my face toward the Lord God to make request by prayer and supplications, with fasting, sackcloth, and ashes.

(Daniel 9:2 & 3)

Daniel began to pray and confess. It was then that he got an answer concerning Israel's purpose. We need to PRAY.

Prayer - communication with the Lord, plays a key role in fulfilling our purpose!

1. **Press or Travail** – When you realize that it is time to birth that dream or purpose, then it is time to travail. Travail means painful laborious effort. In order words it is time to press through the pain or trials you are facing. It is not time to quit or be discouraged. Travail through your prayers. I love the acronym PUSH – Pray Until Something Happens. Push through your pain, push through in prayers, and push through in Praise.

When Praise travails (pushes), it brings forth purpose! "Who hath heard such a thing? ....For as soon as Zion travailed, she brought forth her children." (Isaiah

66:8) Use Praise to help you press through and birth that purpose. **Jesus** (Matthew 26:36-46), **Paul** (Galatians 4:19), **Elijah** (I Kings 18:41-44) and **Jacob** (Genesis 32:24) all travailed. See? It's not limited to women!

2. **Retreat, Rest and Recharge** – Mothers are often advised to get lots of rest while expecting, and considering the amount of pressure one goes through before birthing their dream, the same advice should be taken. Also note that rest and nurture are needed for both mother and baby *after* birthing. Take out some time to spend alone with the Lord, get into His presence and seek his face as regards to your dream or purpose. And after your purpose is birthed, you'll still need time in His presence to rest and to nurture that baby.

Jesus took out time right before he started his ministry (before his purpose was birthed) at thirty years of age; he also spent some time alone in the garden right before his purpose was to be fulfilled. He is also seated at the right hand of the father making intercession for us. (Matthew 4:1-2; Romans 8:34)

When I think of rest, I often think of "catching your breath" and strengthening yourself. A time of spiritual rest does not have to mean sleep or no work. The Bible says that God rested on the seventh day, but we all know that He has not stopped working because He still is! It is a time to Inhale and exhale—to breathe, so as not to get overwhelmed. In school as a young girl, we learned a song that still comes to mind; here are the words, "Rest in Music is a period of silence." As you prepare to birth that dream or purpose, you should take a time of rest—a period of silence—not to fall asleep or be idle but to retreat and rekindle. Also Jesus advised his disciples to come away a desert place to rest.

And He said to them, "Come aside by yourselves to a deserted place and rest a while."... Mark 6:31-32

3. **Act or move** – Have you ever tried to move in a certain direction but each time you experience a closed door? You might think during those times that the enemy is definitely the one responsible for that. However it's not always the enemy; don't be too quick to give him credit. At times God closes door because it is not yet time; He also opens doors when it is time.

After the door has been opened, you might still be faced with adversaries, oppositions, obstacles, fear...but do not allow those hinder you from moving forward. *"For a great and effective door has opened to me, and there are many adversaries." (1 Corinthians.16:9)*

Gideon was faced with fear when was instructed to destroy his father's altar of Baal, but he did it anyway, while still in fear. (Judges 6:27) Go on and do it afraid! Saul was faced with adversaries (rebels) when he was proclaimed King, but he held his peace and did not let that stop him. (I Samuel 10:27)

What is the difference between a door that is shut by the Lord or that which is closed by the enemy? When God shuts a door, no one can open it and when He opens a door, no one can shut it. When God blesses, no one can curse. (Numbers 23:8) If God be for us, who can be against us? As the songwriter put it, when Jesus says yes, nobody can say no.

When the enemy shuts a door, it can be opened if you are in God's will—by prayer, faith, praise and thanksgiving. When you pray, believe, and praise God, and if mountains can be moved then a closed door does not stand a chance.

So Jesus answered and said to them, "Have faith in God. For assuredly, I say to you, whoever says to this mountain,

'Be removed and be cast into the sea,' and does not doubt in his heart, but believes that those things he says will be done, he will have whatever he says. Therefore I say to you, whatever things you ask when you pray, believe that you receive them, and you will have them. (Mark 11:22-24)

4. **Yield or submit to God** - Do not fight against His will. It might not be something you want to do or would love to do. However deep within, you know there is a need for you to do it. An expectant mother eagerly awaits the birth of her baby, because her desire is to see and hold her baby. In the same way, we do should not fight against God's will but embrace it because we want to see and hold our babies—our dreams. When your time comes, yield and submit to God's will. This is just another benefit of doing God's will.

"*Now we know that God does not hear sinners; but if anyone is a worshiper of God and **does His will**, He hears him.*" (*John 9:31*).

Jesus prayed for God's will. (*Matthew 6:10, Matthew 26:39*). We therefore should always pray for His will.

A couple of years ago, I went through a program for my teaching certification. On the first day we were warned of the challenges we were going to face. We were given lots of advice on steps we could take to be successful. Although I had heard about this particular program in the past, I hadn't enrolled until this time around. Everything seemed to fall into place—from turning in the application on time, to being accepted into the program; from getting the finances needed and getting time off, then going through the actual program.

The difficulty of the program was not underestimated— some people dropped out—but I knew that dropping out was not an option for me. I had to press and push both my spirit and flesh! Sometimes I had to retreat; I could not do what everyone else was doing and said no to a lot of things. I had to act, and I had to yield in order to successfully complete the program.

My point in sharing this is to make you aware of the importance of timing and moving forward. Realize that when you see those open doors, then IT IS TIME to press through so as to successfully birth that dream.

Jacob **pressed** while he wrestled with the Man and would not let go till He blessed him (*Genesis 32:24-28*); Jesus **retreated** to the mountain for forty days and nights before starting his ministry (*Luke 4:1&2*); Elisha **acted** by steadily following Elijah so as to see him taken up and finally got a double portion of his anointing (*I Kings 19:4-19*); Paul **yielded** when he had an encounter with Jesus, on his way to Damascus to persecute Christians, (*Acts 9:1-7*)

You can birth different dreams at different times, and you can fulfill different purposes at different periods or stages of your life. I heard someone once say that all ministries are dreams, but not all dreams are ministries.

In other words, every purpose is a dream, but not all dreams are purposes!

Furthermore, every purpose is a result of a dream (*or begins with a dream*) but not all dreams are the result of a purpose (or result in a purpose). Sometimes we have dreams as a result of *selfish* purposes—what we feel we want—but those dreams fall by the wayside.

Pain is necessary in every birthing process, but it only comes for a season. I ran away from pain for a while, but then realized that in order to grow or move to my next level in God, I had to go through pain. Although I did not like pain, I had to acknowledge that I was ready to go through it; I was tired of running.

I went through a very painful experience that also led to brokenness in me. I believe it was more painful because it was unexpected. It came suddenly and it caused a lot of sadness and tears. There was no one to turn to except the Lord.

Whenever I prayed, my question was, "Why?" After the initial shock of pain and brokenness, after travailing and seeking, I realized that I was getting ready to birth a purpose—that this situation was a signal that it was *time*.

Pain has a way of pushing us to fulfil our dream. If we do not feel pain we will not be compelled to press or push through till we birth our purpose.

Hannah was provoked severely by her rival. She was so miserable that she wept and did not eat. The Bible says that in the bitterness of soul she prayed to the Lord and wept in anguish, (Read: pain, agony, distress!) In her anguish, Hannah made a vow. As a result of this she was able to birth her purpose -- in the form of her son Samuel whom she gave back to serve the Lord. He became a great priest and the Lord used him mightily as a prophet in Israel.

Are you going through a time of sudden brokenness and pain? If so, brace yourself! Get ready for the birthing of your purpose!

Or it could be that you have not gotten to that stage yet. You might begin to wonder when it will happen.

Do not be discouraged. Only the Lord knows when it is time, and He will let you know! Be sensitive and obedient to the Lord. You will know when it's time, just like the mother and her baby.

Overcoming Obstacles

There will be obstacles when you try to fulfill your purpose. When obstacles come your way, do not be discouraged. Trust God. Many times people stop halfway to the fulfillment of their purpose, and dreams are aborted because of an obstacle.

There is one major obstacle that we face when trying to fulfill our purpose, and it is called *fear*. Fear usually arises due to *unbelief*. Down deep, we don't believe that God will take care of us. Fear comes in different forms: fear of failing, fear of rejection, fear of defeat, pain or hurt...

The children of Israel, when they were finally so close to possessing their Promised Land, missed out because of fear. Several of those sent to scout it out reported that there were "giants in the land." They said the land "devoured" it inhabitants. That report was sufficient to paralyze anyone but Caleb whose trust was in God.

David, too, encountered a giant when he faced Goliath. But because of His trust in God, he was filled with courage. It was his focus on God that fueled him to overcome that huge obstacle.

In the same way, it's the focus on new LIFE that strengthens a mother to keep pushing through her contractions at the time of birth. Talk about overcoming an obstacle! It's not an easy entry we have into this life.

But it's worth it.

Put your trust in God and He will strengthen you to overcome every obstacle—even real giants! Keep your eyes on Him and you will be able to birth your purpose.

EVERYTHING TO GAIN

Hannah, her husband Elkanah and the children of Israel gained so much because of the purpose Hannah birthed through pain.

Jesus went through agony in the garden before He

birthed His purpose. Because of His pain, everyone has access to the gift of salvation, healing and fullness of life..

I believe that you too will be challenged to launch out, and take steps to fulfill the call or dream He has placed within you. If you are struggling with responding to His call, maybe because of fear of losing relationships, know this: God is able to restore relationships. As for your loved ones, they have everything to gain from you obeying His call. If they do not recognize it immediately, just hold on.

In the words of one of my spiritual mentors, spoken to me years ago, **"If you answer God's call for your life and you give your all, you and your loved ones would have everything to gain."**

This statement was the catalyst that propelled me to respond to my calling. Being brought up by strict parents, it was very difficult to go a different way without being viewed as being defiant. I was brought up as a Roman Catholic, so becoming a Born Again Christian was regarded as rebellion. Also being timid did not help matters either. It seemed as though timidity was my middle name! A popular scripture spoken to me was, "For God has not given us a spirit of fear but...' you know it! If only I had a dollar for every time it was spoken to me.

For many years, I kept dreams and desires buried deep within me because I was afraid to offend or lose certain relationships, especially those in my family. I believed the lies of the enemy, that my family and I would miss out on the wonderful things of life. I lived a half-filled life, trying not to offend anyone until the day I got that revelation.

What a life altering statement it was! Not only did I feel like scales had fallen from my eyes, I also felt like the chains that held me bound were broken off. I left that service knowing that I had to live my life to the fullest. I had to do what God had placed in my heart. I could not keep it inside anymore I had to respond to His call which I felt was tugging at me from within. My life has never been the same since that nugget was shared with me. It gave me a breakthrough in my spiritual life. Yes there have been trials along the way, but nothing can be compared to the joy and peace He has given me since I made the decision to be who He created me to be. *To be me to the fullest!* His grace and mercy has truly brought me through!

One more thing: If you find yourself thinking it is too difficult or impossible, you are not alone! However I recently began to view the word "impossible" differently. I see an invisible apostrophe which represents our invisible Lord, the great "I AM." Next time you see the word impossible, instead of thinking of what isn't possible; look at it this way, **I'MPOSSIBLE** – (I AM Possible!) It was spoken by the angel Gabriel: With GOD all things are possible! Be assured that if the Lord put that dream in you, He will be there with you to help fulfill it!

GO BE 'YOU' TO THE FULLEST!

*"I call heaven and earth as witnesses today against you, that I have set before you **life** and death, blessing and cursing; therefore **choose life**, that both you and your descendants may live." (Deuteronomy 30:19)*

Once you have a birth, then what follows is growth and maturity. That's what you have to look forward to.

You were created unique and beautiful! At times you may find that difficult to believe, especially if you've been told for most of your life that you are worthless and will not amount to anything. If you have struggled with rejection in your life, you may not overcome it in one day (except by a miracle—which is possible!) It might be a process for you, just as I've described in this book.

You may receive instant healing just like blind Bartimaeus who suddenly received his sight. (Mark 10:52) Or you may go through a few "washings," like the man who was told to go wash in the pool of Siloam. (John 9:7) Whatever path the Lord has prepared for you to take, it all boils down to this:

Trust in the Lord, walk with Him and never give up.

I heard of a lady who visited a counselor and shared how miserable she was. She talked about how nobody liked her because she was not pretty. On and on she went!

Finally the counselor said to her, "If I were them, I

would not like you either, based on how you have described yourself!" The counselor went on to say, "Obviously you do not like yourself either."

Tough counselor!

If you do not love yourself, it will be difficult to see yourself being loved.

So I would suggest you do this: **Begin encouraging yourself!**

If you already do, keep at it! If you've never tried it, start with scriptures like this:

"I am fearfully and wonderfully made..." (Psalm 139: 14)

"Nothing can separate me from the love of God." (Romans 8: 39)

I would also suggest you think of the Lord as a mirror. The more you look at Him—the more time you spend in His presence—the more He will show you who you are. And the more you will begin to reflect who He is!

He may also reveal things to you that help you become a better you. Those revelations are not given to fix someone else. Neither are they given for you to change who you are. No, they are given to help fix you, so as to become more fully YOU.

Continue to gaze into Him! Continue to declare His truth in your life!

Yes, there will be difficult days. There will be trials. But if you stay in God, there is a guarantee: God always wins!

Trust in the Lord with all your heart and you will discover your steps have been—are being and will be—directed by Him.

As I mentioned in Chapter 6, the Bible says, *"Many are called but few are chosen." (Matthew 20:16)* I used to think the "chosen few" referred to here were "special" ones handpicked by God. It sounded like it was a done deal.

But now with a fresh revelation I believe that the chosen

few are those who have *responded* to His call. Not everyone responds with a willingness to go through the process. As you have seen, the process may not be easy. But those who have said, "Yes Lord—I will do Your will..." Those are the ones who are chosen.

Will you say YES to Him? Will you choose LIFE?

Will you choose to focus on God and follow His will as you go through each day? If so, you will grow and step into the fullness of your purpose. And nothing is more beautiful than you being YOU – to the FULL!

PRAYER FOR SALVATION

Do you feel like there is a void in your life? Do you desire a deeper walk with the Lord? Have you ever felt like there's got to be more? I can assure you that there is more in God. However first things first, we need to reconcile our relationship with the Lord. If you do not have a relationship with the Lord, and you would like to ask Him into your life. You can pray the prayer below; pray in this way.

Lord, I repent of all my sins, please forgive me and cleanse me of all unrighteousness. I believe in your son Jesus. I believe He died for my sins, rose again on the third day and is now seated at the right hand of the Father. I give my life to you and I receive the gift of salvation which you purchased for me with your life. Thank you for your love and sacrifice for me. You are now Lord over my life.

Father I pray for the one saying this prayer. Take control of their life, from today onwards let their life be filled with your peace and joy. Let them live for you and let your will be done in their lives. Give them beauty for ashes, heal them of any pain, hurt and sickness. We give you glory and praise, in Jesus' name we have prayed, Amen.

Prayerful guidelines to finding your purpose:

Do you have a relationship with the Lord? Did you just pray the above prayer? If so, go to God in prayer as His child, and ask Him to help you with your purpose. You can pray along these lines.

- Ask God to reveal His will and purpose for your life in different ways (one way is through your desire so you can begin to want what He wants).
- Seek Him concerning His will, and be ready and willing to accept it.
- Ask Him to help you surrender your will, to His will.

Prayer for Healing and Forgiveness

Do you struggle with unforgiveness. Are you finding it difficult forgiving someone who has hurt you? Are you bitter towards that individual, could it be that they never apologized for what they did to you; or didn't do? Whatever the case maybe. You can use the following guidelines to help you pray about it.

- Pray, that the Lord reveal any unforgiveness or bitterness in your heart.
- Ask the Lord to help you forgive everyone that has hurt you.

Lord, I pray for healing for those reading this, who have been hurt or emotionally scarred in anyway. Reveal any bitterness, unforgiveness or grudge they have hidden in their heart. Maybe they have been hurt by a mentor, a friend, a family member and they have buried it and have refused to visit that pain. Whether it be for days, weeks, months or years, uncover it and help them forgive and let it go so they can move onto the greater things which you have for them. In Jesus' name, Amen!

On behalf of anyone who has hurt you, it could be someone in a leadership role- a mentor, master, mother, father; or someone in a subordinate role- a mentee, worker, child...; a friend, sister, brother...; whether it is a person superior-senior, junior or at the same level with you; I apologize, please forgive them and allow the Lord to take that hurt away and receive His healing.

GOD BLESS YOU!

Printed in the United States
By Bookmasters